BIG HEART
LITTLE STOVE

BIG HEART LITTLE STOVE

—

BRINGING HOME MEALS & MOMENTS FROM THE LOST KITCHEN

ERIN FRENCH

WITH

RACHEL HOLTZMAN

Photography by Nicole Franzen

CELADON
BOOKS

NEW YORK

ALSO BY ERIN FRENCH

COOKING

The Lost Kitchen

MEMOIR

Finding Freedom

BIG HEART LITTLE STOVE.
Copyright © 2023 by Erin French.
Photographs copyright © 2023 by Nicole Franzen.
All rights reserved.
Printed in the United States of America.
For information, address Celadon Books,
a division of Macmillan Publishers,
120 Broadway, New York, NY 10271.
www.celadonbooks.com

Book design by Jan Derevjanik
Food styling by Rebecca Jurkevich
Prop styling by Suzie Myers

Library of Congress Cataloging-in-Publication Data
Names: French, Erin (Chef), author. | Holtzman, Rachel, author.
Title: Big heart little stove : bringing home meals & moments
from the Lost Kitchen / Erin French with Rachel Holtzman.
Description: First edition. | New York : Celadon Books, [2023] | Includes index.
Identifiers: LCCN 2023009117 | ISBN 9781250832313 (hardcover) | ISBN 9781250832320 (ebook)
Subjects: LCSH: Cooking. | Lost Kitchen (Restaurant) | LCGFT: Cookbooks.
Classification: LCC TX715 .F8655 2023 | DDC 641.3—dc23/eng/20230317
LC record available at https://lccn.loc.gov/2023009117

Our books may be purchased in bulk
for promotional, educational, or business use.
Please contact your local bookseller or the
Macmillan Corporate and Premium Sales Department
at 1-800-221-7945, extension 5442, or by email at
MacmillanSpecialMarkets@macmillan.com.

First Edition: 2023

10 9 8 7 6 5 4 3 2 1

FOR MICHAEL,
MY HEART AND MY HOME

CONTENTS

INTRODUCTION

IT WAS THE FIRST SATURDAY OF DECEMBER, THE KIND OF DROWSY WINTER afternoon when evening closes in at 3 p.m. It was bitterly cold outside, but my dining room was made warm and welcoming by the glow of a dimly lit floor lamp and a constellation of candles, plus an oversized secondhand rug that I'd managed to lug up nineteen steps (not that I'd counted) and spread beneath my table made from scrap wood and galvanized sawhorses. In the candlelight, you'd never have guessed that I'd sewn the tablecloth on my grandmother's sewing machine from a bolt of linen-look-alike fabric I'd unearthed at the odd-lot store, and the mismatched dishes—sourced with the last of my savings at rummage sales—looked downright elegant.

In minutes, sixteen people would walk in my front door expecting to be served a meal. It felt like my craziest idea yet, to host a five-course dinner for people I didn't know (except for the handful I'd convinced to come to make for a more respectable showing) with no fine-dining experience, or even a second pair of hands. Just me, my 1992 four-burner GE Electric, the best ingredients I could find, and an overwhelming desire to fill people with the kind of warmth and joy that can only come from food made with love.

I knew in the pit of my being that this was what I was born to do, but still the nerves hit. Hard. My heart hammered as I second-guessed everything I was about to do. I thought that with one look at my tiny apartment and even tinier kitchen, my guests would know I was an impostor. *Who was I to play restaurant?* But then I remembered the still-dewy heads of baby lettuce perched on my counter, waiting to be tossed with crisp fennel and the last of the gem-toned fall fruit I'd managed to score at the market. I pictured the oysters that had been plucked from the ocean that morning, icy and cold and filled with the promise of their salty brine. There was the Calvados sorbet in the freezer to gently stir appetites between courses; the line-caught Maine cod that I'd sear to a crispy golden brown in cast-iron skillets before finishing it in the oven with more butter than I might care to admit; pungent, salty cheese that I'd offer up beside tiny squares of honeycomb and toasts; and the upside-down cornmeal and caramelized pear cake I'd made that morning to be served in generous slabs, dolloped with tangy crème fraîche. I'd deliberately and devotedly made each of these selections and each of the dishes as though crafting an offering more than a meal.

Yes, I knew (hoped) that they would all be delicious, but more than that, I could imagine the *feelings* that they would evoke. From helping guests leave behind the events of the day with a tart, refreshing cocktail and nibbles for grazing to everyone slouching a little deeper in their chairs after a warm bowl of silky potato soup made even more fragrant with herb-infused oil to hands softly brushing hands as they passed around a platter of carefully prepared vegetables harvested that morning to the contented hush that would fall over the table as everyone tucked into their main course and finally to the wide-eyed delight over sweet treats (and unrestrained giggles when these were followed up with a surprise second dessert of freshly baked cookies)—these are the moments I would quilt from uncomplicated, unfussed recipes made and served, quite simply, with love. And no nerves or chipped plates or sorely outdated kitchen appliances would stand in the way of something I knew so deeply, so innately, that I could do.

By the time the Miles Davis playlist had long since run out, the tapers melted and snuffed, the French presses emptied, and the wineglasses drained, and the last guests were shrugging on their coats with a tipsy glow, I knew that after years of feeling like there were no clear signposts on my life's path, I'd found the one that mattered. It was the little chalkboard, the one my mom had dug up from her old teaching supplies, that I'd hung at the top of the staircase to indicate to guests that they were in the right place: it said, "Welcome to The Lost Kitchen."

Over time, I was lucky enough to be able to share my passion with more and more people, first at regular suppers in my apartment, and then eventually filling a restaurant dining room. It wasn't exactly a straight line or simple process (to say the least), but even through hardships and heartbreaks and soul-crushing setbacks, and uncertainty as to whether anything would ever be OK again, the need to connect with people and to nurture them through food that I could make with my own two hands was the driving beat that pushed me through.

For a handful of years, it seemed as if the dust had settled, and I was able to ease into a new rhythm. I was cooking in my beloved mill on Freedom Pond, and my life was quiet and small. Its boundaries were essentially drawn around the tiny town of Freedom, Maine—I never had much reason to leave, as the ingredients I cooked with at my restaurant came mostly from farms I could see from my window. The farthest anything traveled was the coffee and bread I drove three hours round-trip to get every Tuesday from Deer Isle, part of a spray of islands just off the coast. I was living and working in the place that had raised me, every day passing the houses, barns, roads, and people who were sewn into the fabric of my life. It was familiar and quiet, and I liked it that way. As long as I could serve my food with the same intention and care as when I'd hosted my very first supper club, it didn't matter who walked through my door. I didn't mind being just a self-taught cook in her little restaurant in the middle of nowhere.

But along the way, this little restaurant in the middle of nowhere somehow found itself in the international spotlight. While we weren't strangers to a full dining room booked up months in advance, at midnight on April 1, the moment we opened our phone lines for the next season's reservations, the game changed. One news headline read "10,000 calls in 24 hours for a 40-seat restaurant." Our three-line phone system groaned under the weight of all the calls. We couldn't empty the voicemail quickly enough as the requests continued to pour in, to the point that our security system, unable to dial out for hours on end, set off alarms and alerted the fire department. The world had found The Lost Kitchen.

Just like I knew that some things (the integrity of our ingredients, the integrity of our service, the integrity of our commitment to our local community) would never, ever be compromised, even in the face of this surreal boom of visibility, I also knew that other things would have to change. Our reservation system, for one, which now asks hopeful guests to mail us a postcard—a welcome return to the loveliness of handwritten notes that perhaps simultaneously saved the Freedom post office from having to cut back its hours.

I also wanted to figure out how I could find a way for anyone who wanted to partake in this special place to be able to. I saw the thousands of postcards with their heartfelt notes, poems, illustrations, and other personal touches that had not been selected for that season's dinners, and I wanted to build a bigger table, as it were. I wanted to give people a tangible piece of this restaurant that they could take home with them. After all, what will also never change is that I'm still the same girl who just wants to bring guests into my world and take care of them. So I'd like to think of this book as essentially setting a place for everyone at The Lost Kitchen, whether or not you're here in Freedom.

To do that, I've been reflecting on what makes this place so special. To be honest, it's a question I've asked myself over and over again. That's partly because it sometimes mystifies me how a collection of imperfections, mistakes, and lessons learned the hard way could have turned out as they have. But then I remember that the restaurant was never just a restaurant. For one thing, it has never been just a place to work. It is the embodiment of my whole heart and soul. The women who work here are my family, each one contributing her own gifts to round out our village, whether it is growing the flowers we use for the arrangements in the dining room or cultivating the very food we eat or nurturing us all with kindness. The Lost Kitchen is *home*. Every time we open the doors and welcome people inside, it is with the purpose of inviting them to be a part of that. As a result, this kind of sincerity and authenticity has redefined what our guests think of as "restaurant food." You won't find any tweezers, sous vide machines, or culinary degrees here. Many of the dishes that fill the menu come from my childhood memories—things I learned to make on the line at my dad's diner, my mom's specialties that we looked forward to seeing on the table when we got home from school, my grandmother's recipe box classics, and Mainers' rites of passage. The rest are simple preparations that take the lead from what's good and fresh. And the hospitality details that are there every step of the way to delight, to lull, to indulge, and to connect don't come from any restaurant playbook—they come straight out of our own personal kitchens, living rooms, and dining rooms. But more than anything, when we set out to serve our guests a meal, our ultimate goal is not really to serve them food. It's to create those same feelings I set out to capture back in my apartment all those years ago.

What I discovered organically as I slowly made my way from that supper club to cooking out of a converted Airstream in any farm or field that would have me to running my own restaurant is that it may be the promise of a good meal that first brings people in, but it's the intention to make them feel completely comfortable and at ease that keeps them there long into the evening. It's the difference between people saying, "That was an amazing meal," versus exclaiming, "That was an *amazing night*." And the guiding light that makes it possible is this: simple dishes prepared and served with the utmost thoughtfulness and care.

I can tell you with time-tested certainty that when you care so deeply about what you're doing and about the joy and well-being of your guests, that love can be tasted. People can *feel* it. And it's the best ingredient there is. When you prepare meals with love, when you put your entire self into that beautiful effort, you don't need a big fancy stove. You don't need all those kitchen tools. You don't need complicated recipes or expensive ingredients. You just need a handful of back-pocket dishes, the resources around you, and a big heart. At its core, The Lost Kitchen is still that four-burner electric range in my apartment. No matter how far we've come since then, we will always remember our roots and the lessons that got us here—which are now yours to enjoy at home.

At the heart of this book are recipes that can suit any meal, any mood, and any season. They are easy to prepare, easy to personalize, and quick to impress. And they all foster the kind of welcoming, communal spirit that we've become known for at The Lost Kitchen. You'll notice that these dishes are not organized by season, as the recipes in my first book were, but rather by their role in a meal: Nibbles & Sips, Soups & Stews, Salads & Sides, Suppers, Sauces & Staples, Sweets, and Sundays. That's because when I craft a menu, I'm always thinking about the mood that each course will bring to the rhythm of the meal. There are starters to welcome and convene, soups to comfort or cool, salads and sides to share, suppers to settle into, and sweets to spoil. (Seriously, I think your guests should feel like spoiled children at the end of a meal—the reason why we oftentimes serve our desserts with a glass of cold milk.) When I think of the perfect meal, it's one during which our guests are moving through these feelings, alternating between getting lost in their own emotions and connecting more deeply with the people around them. It's a dance at the table between individual and collective experiences, a dynamic back-and-forth that is at once evocative and joyful. That begins with every plate or bowl of food that you serve having a purpose. Ask yourself, *How do I want my guests to feel?* It's a more important question than, *What do my guests want to eat?* Because while a dish that meets the craving for a flavor is certainly part of what makes a meal stand out, a dish that meets the craving for an *emotion* is what imprints that memory forever.

And that doesn't stop with the dishes you serve. It's the plates, the silverware, the music. The smells and sounds. It's that nice, warm bubble that people don't want to leave. In the final chapter on page 239, I've shared some of my favorite "signatures," or subtle touches that create an even more meaningful experience for your guests. For example, you couldn't properly take The Lost Kitchen home with you without learning how to bring the outdoors in. I've always felt the romantic tug of nature, so it only makes sense to include it everywhere I possibly can (not to mention the fact that it is completely free). From covering just about every available surface with flea-market vases bursting with foraged arrangements (flowers, branches, seed pods, moss, you name it!) to finishing my dishes with sprays of edible flowers (what could possibly make a salad or sandwich or scoop of ice cream more special?) to infusing herbs and other seasonal botanicals into teas and simple syrups and using them to give my menu a sense of time and place to nestling my signature offering of oysters into a tray of frozen rocks scavenged from right outside my door—the beauty and pleasure of these experiences is made all the more significant by the care that went into making them possible. And all of these touches are available to you— I promise!—with a little planning and a little resourcefulness (and maybe a little trespassing).

This book will teach you how to tie together all the pieces that add up to singular meals and moments. I talk about what to serve, when to serve it, and how to serve it. I talk about how to make your dining room table/kitchen table/picnic blanket/tree stumps in your backyard the kind of place your guests will want to linger for hours, including all the TLK "hacks" that add that last little *something* your guests won't be able to put a finger on but know in their bones is there. Of course, you don't need to reach for all of these details at once. In fact, sometimes choosing just one or two meaningful gestures goes a long way, like the simple act of offering cold flower- or herb-infused cloths on a hot day (who said all courses had to be edible? See page 269), serving your main course on plates that you've warmed in your oven (a trick I learned from my mother-in-law Julia; see page 277), sending your guests home with small bags of Chocolate Coins with Candied Ginger, Rose & Almonds (page 202), or just serving someone you love a lazy breakfast on Sunday (one of the most effortlessly luxurious things you can do, which is why there's an entire chapter devoted to it; see page 207).

As you move through this book, give yourself the permission and grace to start small and make mistakes. I'll be the first to admit that I've left behind a trail of burned browned butter, underset panna cottas, and rubbery scallops. You shake it off, learn, grow, and move on. (Maybe even have a cry in the pantry.) At the end of the day, what matters most is that you showed up—for yourself and for your guests. When you have a mission to make something special for people you care about, the sear on your steak is almost beside the point (and nothing that a little Roasted Bone Marrow Butter with Chives, page 22, couldn't fix). My hope is that this book will be a jumping-off point for your own creativity and unique touches, and that it will inspire many gatherings to come. It was, after all, made with love.

A COOK'S NECESSITIES

IT'S EASY TO overthink what makes a dish delicious, but the secret is in the basic building blocks: good salt, good olive oil, good vinegar, good butter, and good eggs. When your food is simple, there's nowhere for the ingredients to hide. So stock up on the good stuff. When I refer to any of these ingredients in my recipes, these are specifically what I'm suggesting you use:

SALT: Two big take-aways here: salt matters, and get the big box. For seasoning a dish as it cooks, I always use Diamond Crystal kosher salt. I like the size of the granules and the way they feel in my fingers. Please do not be tempted to use table salt for these recipes; your dishes will turn out way too salty.

For finishing dishes, I use flaky Maldon sea salt. Granted, I am a saltaholic, but I want people not only to *taste* this fresh-from-the-sea saltiness, but also to *see* it flecked over a dish and *feel* the crunch as they eat. I also like haphazardly sprinkling it over many of my dishes because then you end up with hits of little salty bursts, which make the dish more dynamic and interesting and less one-note.

OLIVE OIL: People are always asking me what olive oil I use, so here it is: Greek extra-virgin. I love how it's fruitier and a little softer than Italian oils, and I've never met one I haven't liked. You may need to seek it out in a specialty shop or online (maybe part of why it tastes better?), but the effort is well worth it. And you can get a nice big can of it, because you'll use every last drop. I promise.

VINEGAR: I keep small bottles of white wine and apple cider vinegar stocked in the pantry, but I go for the big mama jug of seasoned rice wine vinegar. It has a little bit of sweetness to it, which mellows the bite of the acid just a notch and helps a dish really shine.

BUTTER: Unsalted. Always. (You can add more salt to a dish, but you can't take it away!) And lots of it.

EGGS: Take this from a woman who is up to her eyeballs in eggs thanks to her brood of thirty chickens: Do Not Skimp on Buying Good Eggs! When they are good and fresh (and ideally from a local farmer who treats their chickens like the lovely little pets they are), your dressings, cakes, and breakfasts will be so much richer and more sumptuous. Also, I let my eggs get to room temperature before using them in most recipes, or I pull them out first when prepping. For more of my (many) thoughts on eggs, see page 231.

SPRINKLING &
DRIZZLING TO TASTE

I'VE ALWAYS BEEN an intuitive cook, one who learned her way around a recipe by feel and instinct. I think that's part of what makes cooking such a satisfying exercise—it's a whole-body sensory experience. In some of my recipes, I call for specific measures for things like salt, pepper, and olive oil because, in those cases, nailing those amounts can make or break the dish, or because it won't be easy to adjust these once the dish is cooked. In others, however, I simply call for seasoning or drizzling to taste. I encourage you to step outside of your comfort zone with this and trust yourself. Over time, you'll understand what a pinch of salt, a couple cracks of black pepper, and a good glug of olive oil can mean for a dish—and it will make you a better cook. Just one word to the wise: start with less, because there's no going back from too much.

NIBBLES & SIPS

TO WELCOME, TO CONVENE, TO CHATTER, TO TOAST

Good Green Olives with
Almonds, Honey & Rosemary 21

Roasted Bone Marrow Butter with Chives 22

Everyday Oysters & Mignonette 25

A Simple Crudo {with a Twist} 29

Pecorino Puffs 34

Farmhouse Garden Whip 35

Roasted Allium Dip 36

Gram's Clam Dip 39

Quick-Pickled Vegetables Two Ways 40

The TLK Nibble Board 43

Sesame & Fennel Nibble Sticks 46

Cheddar & Thyme Nibble Coins 47

Simple Salt-&-Rosemary Crackers 49

Slush Pups 50

Thai Basil Lemonade 52

Fresh Fruit Shrub 53

Lilac Sorbet 56

Apple Cider with Ginger & Rosemary 57

Whether I'm welcoming people into my home or into the restaurant dining room, the very first thing I want to do is put a drink in their hands and something tasty in their bellies, ASAP. Sure, it's hospitality good sense to offer guests some refreshments, but what I'm really after is setting a tone. Anyone who has invited people over, no matter how good of friends they are, can tell you that there's usually a moment when they first arrive that feels a little...stiff, even a little awkward, as everyone adjusts to each other's wavelength and settles in. But offer them a cold glass of Prosecco (maybe poured over a small scoop of Lilac Sorbet, page 56), your favorite cocktail, or a Thai Basil Lemonade (page 52), and suddenly things soften. People feel like they have something to do with their hands; conversation starts to flow. Food also plays a role in that transition, especially if you think of it as an activity. The idea is to keep things feeling comfortable—handheld for your guests, and hands-off for you. I tend to stick with the classics here: great dips with plenty of crisp veggies and crackers, fresh-from-the-oven Pecorino Puffs (page 34), sweet-salty Good Olives with Almonds, Honey & Rosemary (page 21), and, of course, a Nibble Board (page 43). Why reinvent the wheel when you can take mostly store-bought products, complement them with a homemade touch or two, and pretty it all up? These offerings will free you to scurry back to the kitchen to finish up any last-minute prep, while encouraging everyone to find their groove. You'll know you've got it right when the room is filled with laid-back chatter.

GOOD GREEN OLIVES
with Almonds, Honey & Rosemary

A bowl of this perfectly sweet, salty, herbaceous snack is like a munching magnet. People can't resist adding a scoop to their plate, especially alongside a slab of good cheese. And the prep couldn't be easier: drizzle, sprinkle, done.

1 cup large green olives with pits, such as Castelvetrano

1 tablespoon extra-virgin olive oil

2 teaspoons honey

1 teaspoon toasted and coarsely chopped almonds (see Cook's Note)

¼ teaspoon finely chopped fresh rosemary

ADD THE OLIVES TO a decorative dish. Drizzle with the olive oil, then with the honey. Sprinkle with the almonds and rosemary and serve.

COOK'S NOTE: My preferred method for toasting nuts is in a small dry pan over medium-low heat. Toast the nuts, occasionally giving the pan a shake, until they are fragrant, about 1 minute.

ROASTED BONE MARROW BUTTER
with Chives

Butter is my all-time favorite ingredient, and I use an almost shameful amount of it in the kitchen with no regrets. That kind of sumptuous richness is a staple of made-with-love cooking, which is why I also have a soft spot for bone marrow. It's a delicious snack in its own right, especially when pulled bubbling hot from the oven and slathered on grilled bread But I couldn't help but wonder . . . *could it be even better?* The answer to this question is usually, "Yes, with butter," and sure enough, light and fluffy whipped butter folded into bone marrow and accented with fresh chives makes for a decadent, savory treat. Serve this as a starter smeared over grilled bread or, for even more wow factor, allow the marrow butter to slowly melt over a juicy steak.

8 beef marrow bones

1 pound unsalted butter, at room temperature

½ cup chopped fresh chives

1 teaspoon Maldon salt

PREHEAT THE OVEN TO 400°F.

Set the marrow bones on a baking sheet and roast until the marrow is bubbly and browned, about 25 minutes. Let the bones cool until they're comfortable to handle.

Using a butter knife, scrape the marrow into a small bowl. Drain off and discard any excess fat. Let the marrow cool to room temperature.

In the bowl of a stand mixer fitted with the whisk attachment, whip the butter on high speed, scraping down the sides of the bowl as necessary, until fluffy and pale in color, 5 to 8 minutes. Slowly whip in ¼ cup room-temperature water, then add the cooled marrow, chives, and salt and whip for a few seconds to combine.

Transfer the marrow butter to a serving dish or store in an airtight container in the refrigerator for up to 2 weeks.

COOK'S NOTE: You can easily halve this recipe if you're making it for a smaller crowd. Or a treat for one.

MAKE IT YOUR OWN: If you can't find good fresh chives, any soft herbs such as parsley, tarragon, or dill will do. Parsley and tarragon pack more noticeable flavor, so start by adding less than called for and adjust to taste.

EVERYDAY OYSTERS & MIGNONETTE

(each mignonette recipe makes enough for 2 to 3 dozen oysters)

I call these "everyday oysters" because I like showing people that there's no such thing as a "fancy food" that you can only have on special occasions. Actually, though, I'd argue that serving the oysters *is* the special occasion. Served icy cold with a bright, tart mignonette that makes the whole thing taste like the most delicious slurp of ocean, they are nothing short of magical. Far from the typical overbearing cocktail sauce (a no-no for oysters, in this Mainer's opinion), mignonette accentuates the oysters' salty, briny, subtly sweet flavor. Traditionally it's made with vinegar, finely minced shallots, and cracked black pepper, but I've also included a few of my favorite variations that take the whole thing to a more exciting place. You can also flip to page 157 for even more ways to play with this raw-bar staple.

FOR THE MIGNONETTE

¼ cup seasoned rice wine vinegar

¼ cup finely chopped shallots

A few cracks of black pepper

OR TRY ADDING...

APPLE AND THYME

2 tablespoons finely chopped apple
(no need to peel)

1 teaspoon finely chopped fresh thyme

PEACH AND TARRAGON

2 tablespoons finely chopped peach
(no need to peel)

1 teaspoon finely chopped fresh tarragon

CUCUMBER AND DILL

2 tablespoons finely chopped cucumber

1 teaspoon finely chopped fresh dill

STRAWBERRY

2 tablespoons finely chopped strawberry

FOR THE OYSTERS

As many as you want to eat or serve, and the best you can find; I always figure most people will eat 3 or 4, one person won't have any, and some guy or gal will throw back a dozen.

MAKE THE MIGNONETTE: In a small bowl, combine the vinegar, shallots, and pepper, along with any desired mix-ins. Refrigerate to chill, about 1 hour, or up to 1 week in an airtight jar.

-recipe continues-

COOK'S NOTE: Take your time chopping the ingredients. This sauce is so simple that the extra attention paid to perfectly minced shallots (and vegetables or fruit) will make a slight but worthwhile difference.

SHUCK AND ARRANGE THE OYSTERS: You could have them shucked by your fishmonger, as my mother-in-law does, getting them boxed up nice and neatly. Or you could put a little elbow grease into it:

First, remember that oysters are living creatures. Do not suffocate them by storing them in an airtight container. Keep them refrigerated in a bowl covered with a clean, damp cloth until you're ready to shuck. Properly stored oysters can keep for over a week in the fridge.

YOU WILL NEED

Rough brush or towel for cleaning

Oyster knife

Metal mesh glove (optional)

Clean towel

Chilled platter

Crushed ice (page 273), moss (page 255), and/or frozen rocks (page 274)

CLEAN THE OYSTERS: Scrub them under cold running water using a rough brush or towel to remove mud and debris from their shells. You will notice that one side of each oyster is rounded and the other is flatter. The rounded side is the bottom and the flat one is the top—the shell that you'll be removing. The "point" of the oyster, or the place where the two shells meet to form a point—also called the "hinge" or "key"—is, not surprisingly, the key to getting into the oyster.

Before you pick up an oyster knife, remember that even though it doesn't look like other knives in your kitchen, it's still sharp. Take your time and use good sense just as you would with any other kitchen task that has the potential of injury. A mesh glove will lend extra protection for slips, but it's by no means necessary. A kitchen towel will also offer some protection.

Put one oyster rounded side down on a clean folded towel with the key of the oyster pointing toward your dominant hand. Fold the towel up over the non-key end of the oyster and keep your other hand securely across the towel and oyster. Position the tip of your oyster knife directly at the oyster's key. Gently begin working the knife into the key, angling the blade down into the cup of the bottom oyster shell, rocking it back and forth a bit, discarding any debris as it comes loose. When you feel the key give and the knife sink in, twist it as if you were turning a key in an ignition until you feel the hinge pop.

Loosen the remainder of the shell by running the knife around the inside of the top shell, keeping your knife parallel to the table so that it also detaches the oyster from the top shell. Remove and discard the top shell and run your knife gently under the oyster to detach it from the bottom shell, but leave the oyster in place. Bring the shell and oyster to your nose and take a sniff: it should smell salty and clean and be plump and surrounded by liquid. Anything else, and it should be thrown away. (When in doubt, throw it out.) Repeat with the remaining oysters.

Pull out your platter and cover the bottom with crushed ice, some frozen rocks, and/or a scattering of moss. Arrange the oysters on top, taking care not to spill any of their precious juices. Serve with the mignonette, spooned over the top or alongside, and some bubbles. (Champagne or a nice, minerally Chablis goes really well.)

A SIMPLE CRUDO
{with a Twist}

Crudo is a preparation as refreshingly simple as its name. The word *crudo* is Italian for "raw," and crudo calls for fresh raw seafood to be sliced thin and bathed in vinegar and olive oil with a kiss of citrus. Especially when served on a chilled dish, it's a beautifully gentle way to start a meal. You could stop there with this classic version, or you could turn up the volume a little bit with fresh herbs, flowers, and even fresh fruit—one of my favorite ways to unexpectedly highlight the natural sweetness and salinity of the seafood.

1 teaspoon finely chopped shallots

1 teaspoon seasoned rice wine vinegar

4 ounces raw fish or seafood, such as halibut, tuna, or scallops, cut into ⅛-inch slices

1 teaspoon extra-virgin olive oil

Juice of ½ small lemon

Maldon salt, for sprinkling

Edible flowers, for garnish (optional)

PUT A SMALL PLATE in the freezer to chill.

In a small bowl, combine the shallots and vinegar. Let sit for 15 minutes to marinate and soften the shallots.

Arrange the sliced fish or seafood on the chilled plate. Spoon the shallots and vinegar over the fish, drizzle with the olive oil and lemon juice, and finish with a pinch of Maldon salt. (If you're using scallops, taste them first to make sure they need the salt.) Finish with flowers, if using, and serve immediately.

-recipe continues-

COOK'S NOTE: The quality of your fish or seafood is everything to this dish, so don't compromise. If in doubt about your local fishmonger's selection, go with frozen—it's often flash-frozen at peak freshness shortly after it's caught. If you are able to source scallop shells, use them as serving vessels along with some crushed ice, which you can make by pulsing ice cubes in your food processor. Don't forget to chill your serving dish in the freezer ahead of time!

SCALLOP CRUDO
with Peaches

1 teaspoon finely chopped shallots

1 teaspoon seasoned rice wine vinegar

4 ounces scallops, cut into ⅛-inch slices

1 tablespoon finely diced peaches
(no need to peel)

1 teaspoon Fresh Herb Oil (page 160),
made with basil

Juice of ½ small lemon

Edible flowers, for garnish (optional)

PUT A SMALL PLATE in the freezer to chill.

In a small bowl, combine the shallots and vinegar. Let the mixture sit for 15 minutes to marinate and soften the shallots.

Arrange the slices of scallops and the peaches on the chilled plate. Spoon the shallots and vinegar over, drizzle with the basil oil and lemon juice, and sprinkle with flowers, if using. Serve immediately.

HALIBUT CRUDO
with Violet Vinegar

1 teaspoon finely chopped shallots

1 teaspoon seasoned rice wine vinegar

4 ounces halibut, cut into ⅛-inch slices

1 teaspoon Floral Vinegar (page 158),
made with violets

Juice of ½ small lemon

Pinch of Maldon salt

Minced fresh chives, for garnish

Edible flowers, for garnish (optional)

PUT A SMALL PLATE in the freezer to chill.

In a small bowl, combine the shallots and vinegar. Let the mixture sit for 15 minutes to marinate and soften the shallots.

Arrange the slices of halibut on the chilled plate. Spoon the shallots and vinegar over, drizzle with the violet vinegar and lemon juice, and sprinkle with the Maldon salt, chives, and flowers, if using. Serve immediately.

-recipe continues-

TUNA CRUDO
with Ripe Cantaloupe & Lime

1 teaspoon finely chopped shallots

1 teaspoon seasoned rice wine vinegar

4 ounces tuna steak, cut into ⅛-inch slices

1 tablespoon finely diced cantaloupe

1 teaspoon extra-virgin olive oil

Juice of ½ lime

Pinch of Maldon salt

Edible flowers, for garnish (optional)

PUT A SMALL PLATE in the freezer to chill.

In a small bowl, combine the shallots and vinegar. Let the mixture sit for 15 minutes to marinate and soften the shallots.

Arrange the slices of tuna and the cantaloupe on the chilled plate. Spoon the shallots and vinegar over, drizzle with the olive oil and lime juice, and sprinkle with the Maldon salt and flowers, if using. Serve immediately.

PECORINO PUFFS

Toasty on the outside, soft and warm on the inside, these salty cheese-spiked treats are a perfect complement to any cocktail. I like to make the batter a few hours ahead of guests arriving and have it ready to pipe out and pop into the oven so the puffs can be served fresh and hot once everyone's got a glass in hand.

1 cup whole milk

8 tablespoons (1 stick) unsalted butter

1 teaspoon kosher salt

Freshly ground black pepper

A few grates of fresh nutmeg

1 cup all-purpose flour

4 large eggs

½ cup grated pecorino cheese

PREHEAT THE OVEN TO 400°F. Line two baking sheets with parchment paper and set aside.

In a medium saucepan, combine the milk, butter, salt, a few grinds of pepper, and the nutmeg and bring to a slow boil over medium heat. Give the pan a stir and continue stirring as you add the flour. Stir vigorously for about 20 seconds, until the dough comes together. Increase the heat to high and stir just long enough to cook off the raw flour, about another 10 seconds. Remove the pan from the heat.

Transfer the dough to the bowl of a food processor. With the processor running, add the eggs one at a time, waiting until each egg is well incorporated before adding the next. Add the cheese and pulse until combined.

Transfer the batter to a piping bag fitted with a plain round tip. Pipe dollops of the batter about 1 inch tall and 1 inch wide onto the prepared baking sheets, spacing them about 2 inches apart.

Bake until puffed and golden, about 12 minutes. Serve immediately.

FARMHOUSE GARDEN WHIP

Creamy, bright, and fresh, this addictive dip is especially nice in the summer when your garden is bursting with herbs. I love the combination of mint, basil, and dill, but the tangy cream cheese–goat cheese base is so versatile that any herb blend will work. Then all you need are some sliced veggies or crackers for dipping.

8 ounces plain cream cheese, at room temperature

½ cup fresh goat cheese, at room temperature

¼ cup sour cream

2 tablespoons freshly grated pecorino cheese

1 garlic clove, finely minced

2 teaspoons finely chopped fresh dill

2 teaspoons finely chopped fresh mint

2 teaspoons finely chopped fresh basil

2 teaspoons finely chopped fresh chives

½ teaspoon freshly ground black pepper

IN THE BOWL OF a stand mixer fitted with the paddle attachment, combine the cream cheese, goat cheese, and sour cream. Beat on medium-high speed until the mixture is fluffy, 3 to 4 minutes, scraping down the sides of the bowl as needed. Add the pecorino and garlic and beat for 1 minute, just to combine. Add the dill, mint, basil, chives, and pepper and beat to combine.

Serve with crackers or crudités.

ROASTED ALLIUM DIP

This dip is straight-up born from my childhood Lipton French Onion Soup flavor packet dreams. My mom always had a box in her pantry, and it was the beloved staple for many a picnic or potluck spread. Don't be fooled by the chive blossoms here—this dip may be more "refined" in execution, but it is a loyal homage to its humble roots.

4 tablespoons unsalted butter

4 large shallots, thinly sliced

1 small yellow or white onion, sliced

2 tablespoons packed brown sugar

Kosher salt

1 garlic clove, minced

8 ounces plain cream cheese, at room temperature

½ cup mayonnaise

¼ cup sour cream

1 heaping tablespoon chopped fresh chives

Freshly ground black pepper

Chive blossoms, for garnish

IN A MEDIUM SAUCEPAN, melt the butter over low heat. Add the shallots, onion, brown sugar, and a sprinkle of salt and cook, stirring occasionally, until the shallots are well caramelized, 25 to 30 minutes.

Add the garlic and cook, stirring, for 1 minute. Remove the pan from the heat and let the mixture cool completely.

Transfer the shallot mixture to a cutting board and coarsely chop it.

In the bowl of a stand mixer fitted with the paddle attachment, whip the cream cheese on medium-high speed until light and fluffy, 3 to 4 minutes. Add the mayonnaise, sour cream, cooled shallot mixture, and chives and mix until well combined. Season with salt and pepper to taste.

Serve in a decorative bowl, garnished with chive blossoms, with grilled bread, crudités, and/or crackers.

GRAM'S CLAM DIP

Sometimes it's the nostalgia of a dish, not the ingredients themselves, that makes the magic on the table. It's dishes that remind us of loved ones long gone or memories so special that just one bite invites them to wash over us. This is one of those dishes. The dip is a heartfelt reminder of my grandmother, who was a strong proponent of the impromptu afternoon chip 'n' dip and would often throw together a batch of this in a Tupperware bowl. There wasn't a fresh clam to be found in her recipe—it was all canned, all the time. Could I make it more "elevated"? Maybe. But it just wouldn't taste like my Gram's, or the memories she created with her food, which was as unfussy as it gets, and just as good as anything more refined. Go with canned clams and don't look back. Serve the dip with plain ol' potato chips, and you're guaranteed to have a licked-clean bowl, just like Gram's.

8 ounces plain cream cheese, at room temperature

1 cup sour cream

1 teaspoon finely minced garlic

1 (6-ounce) can chopped clams, drained, 1 tablespoon of the juice reserved

1 tablespoon Worcestershire sauce

2 teaspoons fresh lemon juice

1 teaspoon Maldon salt

Freshly ground black pepper

Pinch of cayenne pepper

1 tablespoon minced fresh chives

IN THE BOWL OF a stand mixer fitted with the paddle attachment, beat the cream cheese on medium-high speed until light and fluffy, about 2 minutes. Add the sour cream and garlic, beating until fluffy. Scrape down the sides of the bowl with a rubber spatula as needed. Add the clams, the reserved clam juice, the Worcestershire sauce, and lemon juice and mix on low speed to combine well. Season with salt, black pepper to taste, and the cayenne pepper.

Transfer the dip to a serving bowl, sprinkle with the chives, and serve with chips. The dip will keep in an airtight container in the refrigerator for 3 to 5 days.

QUICK-PICKLED VEGETABLES TWO WAYS

Pickled vegetables are a welcome addition to any appetizer spread because they play nicely with cocktails and cheeses, plus that bright pickled pop really opens up the appetite. For this recipe, I give you two options: perfectly classic, for satisfyingly straightforward and crunchy pickled cucumbers, and a ginger-infused brine that gives you a hit of surprising warm heat. I really like that version with carrots and cauliflower—but hey: your kitchen, your vegetables!

Classic Pickled Cukes

MAKES ABOUT 3 CUPS

1 pound baby or Persian cukes, halved or quartered lengthwise, depending on size

1 tablespoon kosher salt

2 cups ice cubes

1 small shallot, thinly sliced

2 garlic cloves

¼ cup fresh dill

1 head fresh dill blossoms (optional)

1 cup seasoned rice wine vinegar

IN A MEDIUM BOWL, toss the cucumbers with the salt and ice. Refrigerate for 30 minutes to draw out the moisture in the cucumbers.

In a colander, rinse the cukes with cold water and transfer them to a medium-to-large jar. Top with the shallot, garlic, dill, and dill blossoms, if using. Add the vinegar and ½ cup water.

Let the pickles sit for at least few hours in the refrigerator for the flavors to infuse. These will keep in the fridge for up to 2 weeks.

-recipe continues-

Ginger-Pickled Carrots & Cauliflower

2 cups ice cubes

½ cup kosher salt

3 cups cauliflower florets or
3 cups peeled carrots cut into
roughly 3 x ½-inch sticks

¾ cup white vinegar

½ cup seasoned rice wine vinegar

¼ cup peeled and thinly sliced
fresh ginger

2 tablespoons granulated sugar

4 strips clementine or orange zest

2 small dried hot chiles
(I like chiles de árbol)

1 garlic clove, sliced

1 teaspoon mustard seeds

¼ cup fresh clementine or
orange juice

FILL A LARGE BOWL with the ice and cold water and set aside.

In a large pot, combine 12 cups (3 quarts) water with the salt and bring to a boil over medium-high heat. Add the cauliflower or carrots and blanch for about 20 seconds. Immediately drain the vegetables and transfer them to the ice bath. Let them sit for a minute or so to cool, then drain again and transfer to a heatproof bowl. Set aside.

In a small saucepan, combine the white vinegar, rice wine vinegar, ginger, sugar, clementine or orange zest, chiles, garlic, and mustard seeds and bring the mixture to a boil over medium-high heat, stirring until the sugar has dissolved. Remove the pan from the heat and stir in the clementine or orange juice.

Pour the hot brine over the vegetables, then let the mixture cool completely, uncovered, stirring occasionally.

Cover the pickles and refrigerate overnight for the flavors to marry. Transfer the pickles and their brine to an airtight jar and store in the refrigerator for up to 2 weeks.

COOK'S NOTE: I like using clementine juice and zest for these pickles because of their pronounced floral sweetness, but orange zest and fresh-squeezed orange juice will work just fine!

THE TLK NIBBLE BOARD

I go out of my way to incorporate classic gestures of hospitality straight out of the dinner-party playbook. One of my favorites—and a favorite of our guests—is the nibble board, a spread of easily munched snacky bits that pair well with greetings and cocktails. There's no set prescription for what might appear on one of these boards, and I'm not gonna throw a whole bunch of cheese rules at you—I don't like cheese rules (or any rules, really). But one guideline I do abide by is to include at least one element that's homemade. It could be Nibble Sticks or Nibble Coins (recipes follow), fresh chèvre folded with your favorite herbs or spices, or olives that you've tossed with fresh herbs and nice olive oil. It doesn't have to take more than a minute or two, but the thoughtfulness will elevate the whole situation.

OTHER GENERAL (NON-RULE!) GUIDELINES INCLUDE:

SOMETHING CHEESY—Most people will appreciate a selection of the host's favorites. Just don't cut corners here. Cheese is next to butter in my world; it's so important to get it right, and to use a lot of it. I love soft cheeses in the spring because of all the fresh milk available then, and aged cheeses in the winter.

SOMETHING CRUNCHY—Such as Cheddar & Thyme Nibble Coins (page 47), Sesame & Fennel Nibble Sticks (page 46), or another cracker-type item.

SOMETHING SALTY—Olives and other pickled things do nicely here.

SOMETHING MEATY—Such as cured meats, if you're so inclined.

SOMETHING SWEET—For balance; dried or fresh fruit does the trick.

OR, MAKE IT REALLY EASY—Put out a bowl of frozen grapes (with the bunches trimmed into individual serving portions—such a nice way to cool down when it's hot), sprinkle sliced cucumbers with flaky salt, or slather sliced radishes with good butter and sprinkle them with salt. Or keep a jar of jam or a pot of honey and some good cheese in the fridge, and you can have an instant nibble anytime the mood or occasion strikes.

SESAME & FENNEL NIBBLE STICKS

These crispy little breadsticks with a hint of fennel and orange add a touch of from-scratch love to any spread. They are leaps and bounds better than anything that's been sitting on the store shelf (though I've been known to grab those in a pinch, because there's not much that good cheese can't save), and they look charmingly rustic bundled up on a platter.

⅓ cup whole milk

2 teaspoons honey

½ teaspoon active dry yeast

2 teaspoons fennel seeds

¾ cup bread flour,
plus more for dusting

1 teaspoon kosher salt

Grated zest of 1 orange

¼ cup sesame seeds

1 large egg

IN A SMALL SAUCEPAN, whisk together the milk and honey and warm gently over low heat until the mixture reaches 95°F. Remove the pan from the heat and pour the milk into a medium bowl to cool slightly.

When the milk is just warm to the touch, stir in the yeast and let it bloom in a warm place until the mixture bubbles and froths, about 15 minutes.

In a spice grinder, grind the fennel seeds until fairly fine. In a small bowl, whisk together the ground fennel, flour, and salt. Add the flour mixture and orange zest to the yeast mixture and mix with a wooden spoon until the flour is incorporated and a dough forms.

Turn the dough out onto a lightly floured surface and knead for 2 minutes. Place the dough in a bowl, cover it with a kitchen towel, and let it rise in a warm spot until doubled in size, about 1 hour.

Preheat the oven to 350°F. Line two baking sheets with parchment paper and set aside.

Lightly flour your work surface and sprinkle half the sesame seeds over it. Lay the dough on the seeds and use a rolling pin to roll it into a 6 x 14-inch rectangle. (Longer if you can swing it, for nice thin sticks!)

In a small bowl, whisk the egg with 1 teaspoon water and brush half the egg mixture over the top of the dough. Sprinkle the remaining sesame seeds all over the dough and press them lightly into it. Slice the dough lengthwise into ⅛-inch strips (a pizza cutter works well here), then gently stretch each strip out another 2 inches. (This will help your dough get nice and thin.)

Place the strips on the prepared baking sheet a ½-inch apart and bake until lightly golden, 20 to 25 minutes.

Allow the sticks to cool completely on the pan before storing in an airtight container for up to 1 week.

CHEDDAR & THYME NIBBLE COINS

Could you go to the store and buy a box of crackers to serve on your cheese board? Absolutely. Far be it from me to stand between you and a good snack. But trust me, these savory, buttery, crumbly coins are always the standout nibble board addition, and they take barely any time to slice and bake once you have the dough prepped. (Which, by the way, you can stash in your fridge for any time company, or the mood for nibbling, comes a callin'.)

1½ cups all-purpose flour, plus more for dusting

½ cup whole wheat flour

1 tablespoon granulated sugar

1 tablespoon fresh thyme leaves

1½ teaspoons kosher salt

1 teaspoon baking powder

1½ cups shredded cheddar cheese

8 tablespoons (1 stick) chilled unsalted butter, cut into tablespoon-sized pieces

2 large egg yolks

IN THE BOWL OF a food processor, combine the all-purpose flour, whole wheat flour, sugar, thyme, salt, and baking powder and pulse to mix. Add the cheese and butter and pulse to combine. Add the yolks and pulse until a rough dough forms.

Turn the dough out onto a lightly floured surface. Divide the dough in half and roll each half into a log that's roughly 1½ inches thick. Wrap the logs in plastic wrap and chill for at least 4 hours, or for up to 2 days.

Preheat the oven to 350°F. Line two baking sheets with parchment paper and set aside.

Slice the dough into ¼-inch coins and place them on the prepared baking sheets 1 inch apart. Bake until the coins are golden brown, 12 to 15 minutes. Remove from the oven and cool on the baking sheets for 10 minutes. Transfer the coins to racks to cool completely.

These will keep in an airtight container at room temperature for up to 1 week.

SIMPLE SALT-&-ROSEMARY CRACKERS

MAKES ABOUT 50 CRACKERS

Just your basic crackers—and it's the unfrilly, unfussy, matter-of-factness of them that makes them so dang good. They go with just about any cheese, cured meat, or spread you're offering, and they'd be just as at home alongside soup. But despite their rugged workhorse appeal, they're still going to make whatever you serve them with feel a little more polished.

1 teaspoon granulated sugar

1 teaspoon active dry yeast

2 tablespoons extra-virgin olive oil, plus more as needed

1½ cups all-purpose flour, plus more for dusting

1 tablespoon roughly chopped fresh rosemary

1 teaspoon kosher salt

Maldon salt, for sprinkling

IN A MEDIUM BOWL, combine the sugar and yeast with ⅓ cup warm water. Set aside in a warm place, such as near the stove or in a turned-off oven, for 10 minutes, or until bubbly.

Whisk the olive oil into the yeast mixture, then use a fork to mix in the flour, rosemary, and kosher salt. Using your hands, work the dough until it comes together. Turn the dough out onto a lightly floured work surface and knead until it is smooth and no longer tacky, 3 to 4 minutes. If necessary, add a smidge more water, a teaspoon at a time, until you reach this consistency.

Lightly coat a medium bowl with olive oil. Add the dough, cover with a clean towel or plastic wrap, and let the dough rest in a warm spot for 30 minutes.

Preheat the oven to 350°F.

I like to use a pasta roller to get the dough thin and even; roll it through the machine until you reach the number 4 setting. Alternatively, use a rolling pin on a lightly floured surface to roll the dough as thin as you can, ideally paper-thin.

Cut the dough into organic 4 x 1-inch rectangle-ish shapes. Keep your crackers looking a bit imperfect; you don't want them to look store-bought after all that work! Arrange the crackers on two ungreased baking sheets, leaving about 1 inch between them. Prick them all over with a fork, brush them lightly with olive oil, and sprinkle with Maldon salt.

Bake the crackers until golden, about 8 minutes. You may want to rotate the pans halfway through baking if the crackers on one side of the pan begin to brown too quickly. Allow them to cool completely.

Store the crackers in an airtight container at room temperature for up to 1 week.

SLUSH PUPS

When I was little, my grandparents ran a convenience store in Belfast. And, like any proper convenience store in Maine, it had a giant slushy machine with the signature cherry-red and electric-blue offerings. Every once in a while, my parents would treat me to one, and it was always so satisfying: icy and sweet (along with the novelty of having a bright red or blue tongue for the rest of the day). Now that I'm an adult and can have a slushy anytime I want, I like sharing the same delight with guests. We take either our shrub (page 53) or a lemonade base (page 52), pour it into mismatched vintage coupes and dessert glasses filled with ice, and garnish them with something pretty and special. We're going for more of a refined slush pup—a show pup.

COOK'S NOTE: You could make this "recipe" with Thai Basil Lemonade (page 52), or switch up what you're steeping into that sugar syrup, such as lavender, rosemary, thyme, lilac, or ginger.

THAI BASIL LEMONADE

When our guests arrive at The Lost Kitchen in the warmer months, they are always greeted with a glass of something cool and refreshing. I like it to be a beverage that anyone can enjoy, so it's always alcohol-free, and I want it to feel special enough for this big arrival moment they've been imagining since getting the call about their reservation. Since there's nothing that feels quite as touching as tapping into moments from childhood, and there is no more iconic summer cooler than lemonade, I love offering this drink. You can almost see the memories flash across people's faces as they take their first sip, followed by intrigue about what that lovely subtle floral flavor is (the Thai basil). Serve simply over ice, or add a splash of sparkling water, or use it as a cocktail base with your favorite vodka.

1¾ cups granulated sugar

1 bunch fresh Thai basil, stems removed (1 cup packed leaves), plus more for serving

1½ cups fresh lemon juice (8 to 10 lemons)

Ice, for serving

Lemon wedges, for serving

IN A MEDIUM SAUCEPAN, combine the sugar and 4 cups water and bring to a boil over high heat. Give the mixture a good stir to ensure all the sugar has dissolved. Remove the pan from the heat and add the basil. Set aside to steep, uncovered, for 15 minutes.

Strain the liquid, discarding the basil, and transfer to a large jar. Refrigerate until completely cool, about 1 hour or overnight.

Stir the lemon juice into the chilled liquid and serve the lemonade over ice, with a sprig of Thai basil and a lemon wedge to garnish each glass.

FRESH FRUIT SHRUB

A shrub is a regular go-to as one of the late spring/early summer "first sips" that I offer as guests arrive at the restaurant. It's a fermented fruit–based drink with a surprising kick of vinegar that always gives people a moment of pause before they, inevitably, go back for another pull. You can also easily change up this sweet-tart combo with all kinds of different fruits and botanicals—I especially love strawberry, rhubarb, peach, and plum here. Think of it as a way to take a snapshot of whatever is perfectly ripe and in season at the moment, and don't hold back from mixing, matching, and making it your own.

The greatest thing about a shrub, though, is that the concentrate lasts for up to a month in your fridge, so you can have it on hand for anytime you want to make someone—or yourself—feel special. It's minimum effort for maximum impact—and that's just good sense!

2 cups fresh fruit cut into ¼-inch chunks

1 cup granulated sugar

1 cup cider vinegar

IN A LARGE JAR or airtight container, combine the fruit, sugar, and vinegar. Seal and refrigerate for at least 4 days, and up to 1 week, for the flavors to infuse.

Strain the shrub through a fine-mesh sieve into a clean jar. Use a spoon or spatula to press the fruit to extract any juice, then discard the fruit. Store the base in the fridge until ready to serve.

To serve, fill 8-ounce glasses (or smaller ones, if you want a petite pre-dinner sip) with ice. Add 3 tablespoons of the shrub to each glass, top off with sparkling water, give it a stir, and enjoy.

SORBET:
A FANCY NOT-SO-FANCY
PALATE CLEANSER

When I was a little girl, my father once explained to me the difference between our greasy spoon diner and a fancy restaurant. I had never known that any other food besides diner food existed, so this was fascinating to me. "You see," he said, "a fancy restaurant serves sorbet. But not like after dinner, not for dessert. For an *appetizer.*" I pictured the giant creamy scoops of construction cone–orange sherbet we served at our dairy bar window being offered as a treat *before dinner was even served*, and my mind was blown.

Now that I'm all grown up with a restaurant of my own, I serve a small scoop of sorbet every evening—that's right, before dinner. It's a really simple preparation that manages to feel sophisticated and like a trip to the dairy bar all at once. The volume in the dining room goes up by a few decibels with the excitement around the unexpected treat, which not only cools and cleanses the palate but also builds anticipation for what's to come.

The really fun part of this recipe is using surprising flavors to infuse the sorbet base. Lilac is particularly lovely and floral, but you can get as creative as you want with fresh herbs, fruits, or foraged edible botanicals (see Signatures on page 239 for suggestions).

Lilac Sorbet

I take every opportunity I can to bring more of the wild outside into the kitchen, whether it's by adding a wisp of smoke with cedar and pine, giving moody edginess to a dish with foraged bitter greens, or, my very favorite, capturing the romance of edible flowers. Among the closest to my heart is lilac, which many people are surprised to learn is edible. In Maine, wild lilac shrubs line the roads, and for a fleeting two weeks in the spring, I can roll down my window, inhale deeply, and be transported back to my childhood, running barefoot through fields and forests. There's something about experiencing the taste of such a distinctive, evocative smell that makes people's eyes light up. It's truly a food epiphany moment. And if you aren't able to find lilacs, this sorbet is the perfect base for showcasing any flavor that you wish you could linger over for just a moment longer.

1 cup granulated sugar

2 cups lilac blossoms, any stems removed and blossoms lightly rinsed

¼ cup fresh lemon juice

IN A SMALL SAUCEPAN, combine the sugar and 1 cup water and bring to a rolling boil over medium-high heat; remove the pan from the heat. Stir in the lilac blossoms and let sit for 20 to 30 minutes for their flavor to steep.

Strain the liquid into a medium bowl and discard the flowers. Once the liquid has cooled, add the lemon juice. The syrup will turn pink.

Transfer the syrup to an ice cream machine and churn until frozen and smooth. Pack the sorbet into an airtight container and freeze; it will keep in the freezer for up to 1 month.

COOK'S NOTE: Top a scoop of sorbet with a splash of Prosecco, and you have a festive sip to start the evening.

MAKE IT YOUR OWN: The beauty of a basic sorbet is that it is easily adaptable and the sky's the limit when it comes to flavors. Feel free to replace the lilac blossoms with any of the following: 1 cup fresh Thai basil leaves • 1 bag black tea • A handful of fresh lavender flowers • ¼ cup chopped fresh ginger

APPLE CIDER
with Ginger & Rosemary

Toward the end of our season, when summer seems to turn on a dime into fall, our evening ritual of handing guests a drink is no longer about capturing fresh bursts of summer fruit but about embracing the deeper, moodier flavors of autumn. And with the nearby apple orchards beginning to harvest their crops and press their cider, there's no better base for a cold-weather cocktail. I add a hint of ginger for warmth and rosemary for its piney fragrance, plus a nip of good whiskey for anyone who wants to partake, which brings a little extra rosy glow to the cheeks (and feels a tiny bit naughty, like sneaking a flask into the state fair). That said, this drink is just as delicious without the spirits.

FOR THE GINGER SIMPLE SYRUP

½ cup granulated sugar

A 2- to 3-inch knob fresh ginger, peeled and sliced

FOR THE DRINK BASE

1 cup crushed ice (see page 273)

½ cup fresh apple cider

1 ounce good whiskey (optional)

1 sprig fresh rosemary

MAKE THE SYRUP: In a small saucepan, combine the sugar and ½ cup water and bring to a boil over medium heat, stirring to dissolve the sugar. Add the ginger, remove the pan from the heat, and let the mixture steep to infuse the ginger, 15 to 20 minutes.

If you want to make this ahead, cool it all the way down and store it in an airtight container in the refrigerator for up to 2 weeks.

Make the drink: Fill an 8-ounce glass with the crushed ice. Add 1 tablespoon of the ginger syrup, the cider, and whiskey, if you wish. Stir to combine. Garnish with the rosemary sprig and serve.

COOK'S NOTE: This drink is also tasty served cold over ice. Know that you'll end up with more ginger syrup than you need, but it can be stored in the refrigerator for up to 2 weeks. You could certainly use it to make more of this delicious beverage, but it would also be perfect for freezing into a spicy-sweet sorbet, drizzling over a still-warm cake, or sweetening a mug of tea.

SOUPS
&
STEWS

TO COMFORT, TO WARM, TO COOL, TO REFRESH

Asparagus & Tarragon Soup 63

Golden Tomato & Peach Soup 64

Fresh Celery Soup 67

Toasted Coriander & Carrot Soup 68

Lamb & White Bean Stew
with Mint Pesto 71

Potato & Lentil Soup
with Bacon and Herbs 72

A Chowder of Mussels
with Bacon, Leek & Lime 75

By the time I was fifteen years old, I was at the helm of the busy kitchen line at my father's diner. I had been working there since I was twelve, and I knew the lengthy menu like the back of my hand. I could whip up all the standby dishes—sandwiches, burgers, fried fish baskets, steaks. But I wanted to put my own special touch on one particular menu staple: the soup of the day. I didn't have my driver's license yet, so I walked to the farm stand just down the hill from the restaurant (after breaking into the register to grab some cash) and picked out squash and leeks to take back with me. I roasted it all up, pureed it, and added a pinch of nutmeg, just like my dad had taught me, to deepen the flavor of the squash. I was really proud of that soup. It took about half an hour to get it up on the specials board, because how dare anyone be bothered to alphabetize all the individual letters we used to spell out what was on offer that day, but there it was: Cup for $2.95, Bowl for $3.95. Nobody ordered it.

When I was opening The Lost Kitchen and thinking about the kind of food I wanted to serve, soup was very high on that list. I derive great pleasure from its purity; the way simple, often humble, ingredients become more than the sum of their parts; and how it's the ultimate labor of love—beginning with a well-made stock, judiciously adding each individual layer, salting along the way, infusing the flavors slowly and surely. Then, of course, there's the way it makes you feel—like you're back at your parents' kitchen table after walking home from school in the snow, warming your hands on the bowl. Or like that one sip of chilled soup has soothed every last frayed nerve. Soup can be an unexpected offering at a cocktail party, a sophisticated opener for a multicourse meal, or a casual main event with a hunk of bread. It's safe to say that soup will always be on our menu and that everyone's eating it that night. And there have never been any complaints.

ASPARAGUS & TARRAGON SOUP

I don't know why it took me so long to figure out how well-suited the pairing of asparagus and tarragon is, but my forty-one years were worth it, because now I know, and now asparagus will forevermore be better for it. Here the anise-y notes of the tarragon balance the grassy asparagus in what feels like a joyful celebration of spring. It's the rich, earthy, creamy deliciousness that soup dreams are made of.

2 tablespoons extra-virgin olive oil

1 teaspoon fennel seeds

1 medium yellow or white onion, roughly chopped

2 garlic cloves, roughly chopped

2 teaspoons kosher salt, or more to taste

Freshly ground black pepper

2 pounds asparagus, tough ends removed, chopped into 1-inch pieces (about 4 cups)

4 tablespoons unsalted butter

5 cups Roasted Chicken Stock (page 170) or store-bought low-sodium chicken stock

1 cup packed fresh spinach leaves

Leaves from 1 bunch fresh tarragon (about ⅓ packed cup), plus a small handful for serving

⅓ cup heavy cream

Crème fraîche, for serving

IN A LARGE HEAVY-BOTTOMED POT, combine the olive oil and fennel seeds and toast the seeds over medium heat, stirring frequently, until fragrant, about 1 minute. Add the onion, garlic, 1 teaspoon of the salt, and a few cracks of pepper and stir again. Cook until the onions are translucent, 4 to 5 minutes.

Add the asparagus, the remaining teaspoon of salt, and a few cracks of pepper and stir to coat the asparagus. Stir in the butter, tossing the asparagus until the butter has completely melted. Pour in the stock, bring the mixture to a simmer, and cook until the asparagus is tender yet still crisp, 4 to 5 minutes. Remove the pot from the heat and stir in the spinach and tarragon.

Working in batches if necessary, carefully add the hot soup to a blender and blend the soup until completely smooth. Set a fine-mesh strainer over the pot and pour the soup through it. Stir in the cream and taste, adding more salt and pepper if needed.

Gently reheat the soup if it is no longer hot, then serve garnished with dollops of crème fraîche and tarragon leaves.

GOLDEN TOMATO & PEACH SOUP

SERVES 6

Tomatoes and peaches are one of nature's most impeccable matches. Both really hit their stride at the same time in late summer. And both are sweet but with a hit of acid, one picking up where the other leaves off, like they are finishing each other's sentences. It just goes to show what a beautiful marriage ingredients that come into season together can make.

FOR THE SOUP

2 pounds yellow tomatoes, any type, roughly chopped

2 ripe peaches, peeled, pitted, and roughly chopped

2 tablespoons seasoned rice wine vinegar

2 garlic cloves, peeled

Seeds from ½ small jalapeño pepper (or more, if you like it spicy)

½ teaspoon kosher salt, plus more to taste

2 ears fresh corn, husks and silks removed

FOR SERVING

Extra-virgin olive oil

Juice of 1 lime

¼ cup fresh Thai basil leaves

¼ cup fresh cilantro leaves

1 cup Sungold tomatoes, sliced

Maldon salt

MAKE THE SOUP: Place six soup bowls in the freezer to chill.

In a blender, combine the tomatoes, peaches, vinegar, garlic, jalapeño seeds, and kosher salt and blend until completely smooth. Pour the mixture through a fine-mesh strainer set over a bowl and chill until cold, about 1 hour.

Fill a large bowl with a couple handfuls of ice and cold water and set aside.

Fill a large pot with water and salt it generously. Bring the water to a boil over medium-high heat and drop in the corn. Cook until just tender, 2 to 3 minutes. Transfer the corn to the ice bath to stop the cooking and cool it, 2 to 3 minutes. Remove the corn from the ice bath.

Stand one ear of corn up in a large bowl and use a good sharp knife to zip off the kernels, rotating the ear as necessary. Keep 3 or so rows of kernels intact in about 1-inch sections, and reserve these for garnish. Stir the remaining corn into the soup.

SERVE: Divide the chilled soup among the chilled serving bowls. Float the reserved bits of corn on top, drizzle with olive oil, and top each bowl with a drizzle of lime juice. Sprinkle with the Thai basil and cilantro leaves and add a few sliced Sungolds to each bowl. Finish with Maldon salt and serve.

FRESH CELERY SOUP

Once upon a time, celery saved me. We were prepping for our final night of service one year and had planned on serving a tomato soup, but with the cold curtain of fall having already fallen, there weren't enough tomatoes to work with. Luckily my friends Catherine and Alex at Calyx Farm had a bumper crop of celery, and what started as a backup quickly became the star of the show. Fresh, sweet celery cooked down with aromatics and given decadent body with butter and cream is nothing short of elegant.

1 teaspoon celery seeds

2 tablespoons extra-virgin olive oil

4 cups chopped celery (from about 1 bunch), leaves reserved for garnish

1 cup chopped onion

½ cup chopped carrot

4 garlic cloves, chopped

1 teaspoon celery salt

Freshly ground black pepper

1 cup peeled russet potatoes cut into roughly 2-inch pieces

Kosher salt

5 cups Roasted Chicken Stock (page 170) or store-bought low-sodium chicken stock

4 tablespoons unsalted butter

½ cup heavy cream

ADD THE CELERY SEEDS to a dry heavy-bottomed soup pot or Dutch oven set over medium heat. Toast the seeds, stirring frequently, until fragrant, about 1 minute.

Add the olive oil and stir to coat the seeds and heat the oil. Add the chopped celery, onion, carrot, and garlic and season with the celery salt and a few cracks of pepper. Cook, stirring, until the onions are just translucent, about 5 minutes.

Add the potatoes and season with two good pinches of kosher salt (don't be shy) and a few twists of pepper, then give it all a good stir. Add the stock and bring the mixture to a slow boil. Reduce the heat to low and cook, stirring occasionally, until the potatoes are tender, about 30 minutes.

Remove the pot from the heat and carefully ladle about half of the soup into a blender. Add half of the butter and blend until the soup is completely smooth and creamy. Return the soup to the pot and repeat with the remaining soup and butter. Stir in the cream and taste for seasoning, adding more salt and/or pepper if you like.

Divide the soup among bowls and garnish with the reserved celery leaves.

MAKE IT YOUR OWN: You can easily dress this up by adding a dollop of crème fraîche and a spray of edible flowers, or a tuft of fresh crabmeat, to each bowl. One of my favorite touches is to add a spoonful of brown butter to the bottom of each bowl before ladling in the soup.

TOASTED CORIANDER & CARROT SOUP

While carrots are usually relegated to a supporting role, here they become the subtly sweet star, infused with the bright, citrus-like flavor of coriander. I came up with this combination when one of the farmers I work with had first-of-the-season carrots and some bolted cilantro blossoms, which taste like coriander (understandably, since coriander seeds come from the cilantro plant). I loved the idea of the two, and when I saw the marigold-colored soup in the pot, I knew that this would be a recipe that needed to be written in ink. Like most pureed vegetable soups, it's a cozy lunch or starter served warm, and a nice light meal served cold.

3 tablespoons extra-virgin olive oil

2 tablespoons coriander seeds

2 cups chopped yellow or white onion

2 garlic cloves, minced

2 teaspoons kosher salt, or more to taste

Freshly ground black pepper

4 cups peeled carrots cut into ½-inch chunks

4 tablespoons unsalted butter

2 tablespoons brown sugar

5 cups Roasted Chicken Stock (page 170) or store-bought low-sodium chicken stock

IN A LARGE HEAVY-BOTTOMED POT, combine the oil and coriander seeds and toast the seeds over medium heat, stirring frequently, until fragrant, about 1 minute.

Add the onion and garlic, season with 1 teaspoon of the salt and a few cracks of pepper, stir, and cook until the onions are translucent, 4 to 5 minutes.

Add the carrots, the remaining teaspoon of salt, and a few cracks of pepper and stir to coat. Stir in the butter and toss the carrots until the butter has completely melted. Add the brown sugar and stir until it dissolves. Pour in the stock, bring the mixture to a simmer, and cook until the carrots are just tender, 8 to 10 minutes. Remove the pot from the heat.

Working in batches if necessary, carefully transfer the hot soup to a blender and blend until smooth. Strain the soup through a fine-mesh strainer back into the pot. Taste for seasoning, adding more salt and/or pepper if needed. Serve hot.

MAKE IT YOUR OWN: This soup is really versatile and pairs well with many other flavors and textures. Try garnishing it with a drizzle of honey, a dollop of crème fraîche or yogurt, a sprinkling of sunflower seeds, or a few sprigs of cilantro.

LAMB & WHITE BEAN STEW
with Mint Pesto

Whenever my dad would go out ice fishing, my mom would make a big pot of this stew and take it out to his ice shack. We'd sit around out there, play cards, catch fish, and warm the pot over the fire. Now I make her recipe in my own home, keeping bowls of it warm atop my woodfire stove. To eat it is to feel the contentment of the perfect day.

2 tablespoons extra-virgin olive oil

1 cup chopped yellow or white onion

1 cup chopped celery

2 tablespoons minced garlic

1 tablespoon finely chopped fresh sage

Kosher salt and freshly ground black pepper

1 pound dried navy beans

1 (1½- to 2-pound) bone-in lamb shank

8 cups Roasted Chicken Stock (page 170) or store-bought low-sodium chicken stock

1 cup chopped carrots (no need to peel)

2 teaspoons fresh lemon juice

½ cup Kitchen Sink Pesto (page 162), made with mint

IN A LARGE HEAVY-BOTTOMED SOUP POT, heat the oil over medium heat. Add the onion, celery, garlic, sage, a good pinch of salt, and a few cracks of pepper. Stir to coat the vegetables and cook until the onion and celery become translucent, about 5 minutes.

Add the beans and another good pinch of salt, then add the lamb shank and stock. Increase the heat to medium-high and bring the stock to a boil. Reduce to a simmer and cook until the beans are al dente, 45 to 60 minutes (timing will depend on the age of your beans, so test occasionally).

Add the carrots and continue cooking until the beans and carrots are tender, about another 15 minutes.

Remove the shank from the soup and transfer it a cutting board to cool slightly. Shred the meat from the bone, add it back to the soup, and discard the bone. Sprinkle the stew with the lemon juice and season as needed with more salt and/or pepper.

Ladle the stew into bowls and dollop with the mint pesto.

POTATO & LENTIL SOUP
with Bacon and Herbs

There's something about eating hearty, fortifying lentils that always makes me feel like I'm doing something good for myself. Of course, a nourishing dish should also taste delicious, so I've added salty, smoky bacon for good measure. It can be a meal on its own, or, if you really want to go for it, serve with toasts slathered with Roasted Bone Marrow Butter with Chives (page 22).

4 slices bacon

Extra-virgin olive oil, as needed

1 medium yellow or white onion, diced

1 medium carrot, diced (no need to peel)

Kosher salt

1 head garlic, halved horizontally, plus 2 garlic cloves, minced

6 cups Roasted Chicken Stock (page 170) or store-bought low-sodium chicken stock

1 pound baby potatoes, halved or quartered into bite-sized pieces

1¼ cups Le Puy lentils (also called French lentils)

3 sprigs fresh thyme

2 dried bay leaves

Freshly ground black pepper

½ cup fresh mint leaves

⅓ cup fresh dill

¼ cup fresh chive tips

Juice of ½ lemon

½ cup crème fraîche

IN A LARGE HEAVY-BOTTOMED SOUP POT, arrange the bacon in a single layer and cook over medium heat until crisp, 6 to 8 minutes. Transfer to a paper towel–lined plate to drain. Roughly chop into bits and set aside.

Drain off all but 1 tablespoon of fat from the pot. Add a splash of olive oil and heat over medium heat until the oil shimmers. Add the onion and carrot, plus a healthy pinch of salt, and increase the heat to medium-high. Add the minced garlic and a splash of chicken stock, using a wooden spoon to scrape up the browned bits from the bottom of the pot, and cook until the onions turn translucent, 4 to 5 minutes.

Add the potatoes, lentils, halved head of garlic, thyme, and bay leaves and cover with the remaining stock. Bring to a boil, then reduce to a simmer and cook until the potatoes and lentils are tender, 25 minutes. Remove the thyme, bay leaves, and garlic and discard. Add more salt, if needed, and a few cracks of pepper.

In a small bowl, gently toss together the mint, dill, chives, and lemon juice with a splash of olive oil.

Ladle the soup into bowls, top with the bacon and fresh herb mixture, and garnish each serving with a dollop of crème fraîche.

A CHOWDER OF MUSSELS
with Bacon, Leek & Lime

This is the quinetessential soup of the place I call home, and it's one that I crave year-round. There is little that is more comforting than a bubbling pot of chowder on the woodstove, with a creamy mugful in hand—it somehow makes the shorter days of winter feel longer and lighter. But this is equally well suited for summertime, given its straight-from-the-ocean brine that gets a lift from fresh lime and cilantro. I love serving it with Backyard Biscuits (page 127).

2 pounds fresh mussels in the shell

Extra-virgin olive oil, as needed

4 strips bacon, diced

3 cups roughly chopped leeks

2 cups chopped celery

1 cup roughly chopped onion

2 garlic cloves, minced

Kosher salt and freshly ground black pepper

2 dried bay leaves

1 teaspoon fresh thyme leaves

2 tablespoons all-purpose flour

⅓ cup dry white wine

1 pound russet potatoes, peeled and cut into 1-inch cubes (about 4 cups)

6 tablespoons cold unsalted butter

Grated zest and juice of 1 lime

3 cups whole milk

1½ cups heavy cream

⅓ cup chopped fresh cilantro

PUT THE MUSSELS IN a large bowl and completely submerge them in cold water. Discard any mussels that are open or broken. Drain the mussels.

Place a medium heavy-bottomed pot over high heat. Add the mussels and cook undisturbed for 1 minute. Add ¼ cup water to the pot, cover, and reduce the heat to low. Cook until the mussel shells pop open, about 3 minutes. Remove the pot from the heat and discard any mussels that have not opened.

Once the mussels are cool enough to handle, pick the meat from the shells and set aside in a medium bowl; discard the shells. Strain the delicious cooking juices through a fine-mesh strainer into a medium bowl, stopping just before you get to any sandy bits at the bottom of the pot (discard the sandy bits).

In a large heavy-bottomed soup pot, heat a good drizzle of olive oil over medium heat. Add the bacon and cook just until it begins to brown, about 4 minutes. Add the leeks, celery, onion, garlic, a good sprinkle of salt,

-recipe continues-

and a few turns of pepper. Stir to combine and add the bay leaves and thyme. Cook, stirring frequently, until the vegetables are soft and translucent, 4 to 5 minutes.

Raise the heat a smidge, add the flour, and stir well. Add the wine and stir constantly for a minute. Add the potatoes, another healthy sprinkling of salt, and a few cracks of pepper and reduce the heat to low. Add the cold butter and lime zest, stirring constantly until the butter is completely melted. Add the reserved mussel juices, plus the milk and cream, and cook, stirring occasionally, until the potatoes are cooked through and tender, 15 to 20 minutes. Add the mussels and taste for seasoning, adjusting it as needed.

Divide the chowder among bowls, drizzle with the lime juice, and sprinkle with the cilantro. Serve.

MAKING SOUP SPECIAL

WHEN IT COMES TO SERVING SOUP AT THE LOST KITCHEN, WE'RE ALWAYS thinking outside the bowl. Soup on its own is such a lovely moment, but why not take one tiny, effortless step further to make it downright memorable? One of our favorite presentations is to adorn the bottom of empty bowls with beautiful garnishes like edible flowers, fresh herbs, a dollop of crème fraîche, or a drizzle of brown butter. Then we pour the soup tableside from antique pitchers, teapots, or ladles. This manages to touch all the senses at once—inhaling the aromas of the soup as it is released from its vessel, seeing the garnish being consumed by its velvety surrounds, hearing the *oohs* and *aahs* from around the dining room. Plus, it's interactive and fun. Other things you could try are:

- Serving warm soup in teacups
- Serving chilled soup in copper shot cups or Champagne coupes
- Serving hot, silky soups in flasks in the winter

Another way to make soup one of the most exciting parts of the meal is to serve it alongside a sumptuous little treat that can be dipped or sopped. A still-warm buttery Backyard Biscuit (page 127) or a piece of toast generously smeared with Roasted Bone Marrow Butter (page 22) makes the course—or meal—feel like a complete thought and is at the same time reminiscent of a lovingly packed lunch.

SALADS & SIDES

TO GATHER, TO GIVE, TO SHARE, TO EMBRACE

Napa Wedge with Bacon & Blue Cheese 83

Stewed White Beans with Fried Sage 84

Mediterranean Mess 87

Carrot Salad
with Marinated Apricots & Pistachios 88

Peach & Blackberry Bread Salad 91

Fried Squash Rings with Pear, Dried Cherry & Feta 92

Roasted Potato Salad
with Green Beans, Olives & Herbs 96

Summer Squash Rolls
with Herbed Ricotta & Toasted Hazelnuts 101

Green Beans with Sage, Garlic & Breadcrumbs 102

A Salad of Leaves & Blooms 103

Creamy Polenta 106

Rosemary French Frites 107

Honeyed Beets with Feta & Toasted Pistachios 108

Crispy Cauliflower
with Honey & Hot Pepper Flakes 111

Perfect Potato Puree with Bay Leaf & Thyme 112

Although the following recipes pull from all the seasons and their respective inspirations, they have a few things in common. First and foremost, they are meant to be shared. I like having a family-style moment in a meal, because it takes everyone out of their individual experience and back into the communal space of the table. You have to work together, communicate, and help one another. Not to mention the fact that there is nothing more gorgeous or inviting than a beautiful platter piled high with lettuces or vegetables and all manner of fresh herbs and blossoms. That too is what unites these dishes—they are all celebrations of a moment in time when those ingredients are at their best, minimally messed with, and layered with complementary flavors and textures. The recipes in this chapter can be enjoyed on their own for a light lunch or supper, or paired with a main course for something more substantial.

COOK'S NOTE FOR SALADS: Peeling fruit and vegetables is this cook's preference. A general rule of thumb, though, is if the skin is tender, leave it on, but if it is tough, use a vegetable peeler to remove it.

NAPA WEDGE
with Bacon & Blue Cheese

The classic wedge salad, in all of its overdressed iceberg lettuce glory, will always have a place in my heart. (You can take the girl out of the diner . . .) But for some occasions, I like to doll it up just a bit. For starters, I'll use crisp, mild napa cabbage, which still gives that signature structure to the salad but with much more flavor. As for the rest, I don't want to mess around too much with a good thing—I mean, when you think *wedge salad* you want that tangy, creamy dressing; a generous scattering of blue cheese and bacon; and plenty of black pepper—but I do take it up just a notch with a homemade buttermilk dressing, sweet cherry tomatoes, and a spray of edible flowers.

¼ cup seasoned rice wine vinegar

1 small shallot, sliced into thin rounds

4 strips bacon

1 head napa cabbage

3 tablespoons extra-virgin olive oil

½ cup Simple Buttermilk Dressing (page 159)

1 pint cherry tomatoes, halved

Maldon salt, to taste

4 ounces good blue cheese, cut into wide thin slices

¼ cup chopped fresh chives

Freshly ground black pepper

Microgreens and edible flowers, for garnish (optional)

IN A SMALL BOWL, combine the vinegar and shallot rings and set aside to marinate for 15 minutes for the flavors to meld and the shallots to soften.

In a large cast-iron skillet, arrange the bacon in a single layer and cook over medium heat until crisp, 6 to 8 minutes. Transfer to a paper towel–lined plate to drain. When the bacon is cool, roughly chop into bits and set aside.

Slice four 1-inch-thick rounds from the center of the cabbage; discard the bottom end and top of the cabbage.

Place the rounds on dinner plates and sprinkle with the shallots and vinegar. Drizzle each round with some of the olive oil and a large dollop of the buttermilk dressing. Mound the tomatoes on top and sprinkle with Maldon salt. Add the blue cheese and chopped bacon to the heap and finish with the chives, a few cracks of fresh pepper, and microgreens and edible flowers, if using. Serve immediately.

STEWED WHITE BEANS
with Fried Sage

SERVES 6

This is everything you want in a side dish: it's rich and creamy enough to stand up to a protein, yet the earthy fresh herbs and fried sage keep it from being too heavy or one-note. Plus, buttery toasted breadcrumbs add much-needed crunch. The beans are particularly nice served room temperature with pork chops or loin, but you may also just want a bowlful for a simple supper.

2 cups dried white beans,
such as cannellini or great northern,
soaked overnight and drained

¼ cup plus 1 tablespoon extra-virgin
olive oil

3 tablespoons unsalted butter

¼ cup finely chopped shallots

4 garlic cloves, minced

1 teaspoon kosher salt, or more to taste

4 cups Roasted Chicken Stock (page 170)
or store-bought low-sodium chicken stock

2 dried bay leaves

6 fresh sage leaves

1 tablespoon fresh thyme leaves

1 teaspoon finely chopped fresh rosemary

IN A LARGE CAST-IRON skillet or heavy sauté pan, combine 1 tablespoon of the olive oil, the butter, shallots, garlic, and salt and cook over medium heat, stirring frequently, until the shallots soften and the aromas start to fill your kitchen, 3 to 5 minutes. Add the drained beans, stock, and bay leaves, increase the heat, and bring the stock to a low boil. Reduce the heat and simmer until the beans are cooked through and tender and the stock has reduced a bit, about 30 minutes.

Meanwhile, fry the sage leaves: Add the remaining ¼ cup oil to a small skillet set over medium heat. When the oil begins to smoke, add the sage leaves and fry until the edges start to curl but the color of the leaves is still green, 30 to 45 seconds. Transfer the leaves to a paper towel–lined plate and set aside. If you'd like, reserve the sage-infused oil for drizzling over the beans.

When the beans are cooked, remove the pan from the heat, then remove the bay leaves and discard. In a food processor or blender, puree 1 cup of the hot beans with their cooking liquid. Stir the blended mixture back into the pot, along with the thyme and rosemary. Season with more salt, if desired.

Ladle the beans into a shallow serving dish. Finish with the fried sage and sage oil (if desired), and serve immediately.

COOK'S NOTE: When cherries are in season, I love giving them a quick pickley dip in vinegar. That pop of sweetness tempered by the vinegar is the perfect punctuation in a luxurious bowl of creamy beans. To do this, soak 1 cup pitted and halved cherries in 2 tablespoons seasoned rice wine vinegar while the beans cook. When you're ready to serve, drain the cherries and dot over the top of the beans with the fried sage.

MEDITERRANEAN MESS

If there is one cooking misconception that I wish I could finally bust for good, it's thinking that you need to combine fancy ingredients in a fancy way using fancy techniques to make a dish seem special. Not. At. All. For me, the secret has always been to let the ingredients do all the talking and just get out of the way. When you're using beautiful, in-season produce, there's not a whole lot that you need. This dish is case in point: It's a big ol' pile of fresh-from-the-market ingredients that are given the Mediterranean treatment with feta, fresh herbs, and olives. No cooking and no fussing, but *all* the flavor.

2 medium cucumbers (about 8 ounces; see Cook's Note), cut into ½-inch-wide half-moons

1 pint cherry tomatoes, halved

Maldon salt

⅓ cup mixed olives (such as Kalamata, Niçoise, and/or Castelvetrano), pitted

2 ounces crumbled feta cheese (I'm happy with either sheep's- or cow's-milk feta), crumbled

Extra-virgin olive oil, for drizzling

1 heaping tablespoon fresh oregano leaves

A palmful of small, fresh basil leaves, or torn larger leaves (see Cook's Note)

2 teaspoons fresh thyme leaves

Freshly ground black pepper

Dill blossoms, for garnish (optional)

SPREAD THE CUCUMBERS AND tomatoes on a shallow platter and sprinkle with a pinch of Maldon salt. Scatter the olives and feta on top, drizzle with olive oil, and sprinkle with the herbs and a few cracks of pepper. Garnish with dill blossoms, if you can get them.

Serve immediately.

COOK'S NOTE: Look for unique varieties cucumbers at your farmers' market in the summer when they are in peak season. White and lemon cucumbers make a real statement. Poke around for purple basil too!

CARROT SALAD
with Marinated Apricots & Pistachios

SERVES 6

Pantry staple dried apricots that have been marinated in orange blossom water and spices are a little fruity, a little floral, but still have their naturally bright punch. Paired with a salad of crunchy carrots, they make a versatile side that would work as part of a picnic spread or next to your favorite roast.

FOR THE MARINATED APRICOTS

2 dried bay leaves

1 teaspoon coriander seeds

1 cup dried apricots

½ cup orange blossom water

1 tablespoon granulated sugar

FOR THE DRESSING

3 tablespoons minced shallots

3 tablespoons seasoned rice wine vinegar

Grated zest and juice of 1 orange

Kosher salt and freshly ground black pepper

2 tablespoons extra-virgin olive oil

1 teaspoon ground cumin

FOR THE SALAD

10 carrots, peeled and grated with the fine-tooth blade on a mandoline (about 6 cups)

½ cup toasted and roughly chopped pistachios (see Cook's Note, page 21)

¼ teaspoon ground cinnamon

⅓ cup torn fresh mint leaves

MARINATE THE APRICOTS: In a small saucepan, combine the bay leaves and coriander seeds and toast over medium heat, moving the pan around, until fragrant, about 1 minute. Add the apricots, orange blossom water, and sugar and cook for another minute. Remove the pan from the heat and let the mixture steep for at least 20 minutes. (You can do this step ahead of time and refrigerate the apricots in their syrup for up to 2 weeks.)

MAKE THE DRESSING: In a small bowl, combine the shallots, vinegar, orange zest and juice, a pinch of salt, and a few cracks of pepper. Whisk in the olive oil and cumin and set aside.

MAKE THE SALAD: Chop the marinated apricots into roughly raisin-sized pieces. In a medium bowl, combine the carrots and chopped apricots, then add the dressing and toss to coat. Add the pistachios, cinnamon, and mint leaves, toss gently, and serve.

COOK'S NOTE: I call for using a mandoline here because I think it's the best way to get the thinnest slice on the carrots. It also happens to be an inexpensive kitchen gadget that I find indispensable, so I highly recommend springing for one, if you can. Otherwise, you can spend some time being meticulous with a sharp knife. Or, if you're feeling less fussy, use the large holes of a box grater.

PEACH & BLACKBERRY BREAD SALAD

In my book, bread salads are obsession-worthy. There is something so insanely perfect about chunky, golden croutons that have been plumped by a good soak in a vinaigrette. Add the sweetness of fruit and the crunch of cucumber, plus a handful of fresh herbs, and you've got the side dish of the summer. Make this one a main event by serving it heaped over a bed of arugula with a scoop of fresh goat cheese and a glass of crisp white wine.

FOR THE VINAIGRETTE

3 tablespoons seasoned rice wine vinegar

1 small shallot, finely chopped

⅓ cup extra-virgin olive oil

Freshly ground black pepper (optional)

FOR THE SALAD

2 tablespoons extra-virgin olive oil

4 cups 1- to 1½-inch cubes good bread, such as French or ciabatta

Kosher salt and freshly ground black pepper

4 firm but ripe peaches

1 English cucumber

½ pint blackberries (about 1 cup)

½ cup loosely packed fresh basil leaves, gently torn

2 sprigs fresh tarragon, leaves removed

2 sprigs fresh mint, leaves removed and gently torn

Edible flowers, such as pansies or nasturtiums, for garnish (optional)

MAKE THE VINAIGRETTE: In a small bowl, combine the vinegar and shallots and set aside to marinate for 15 minutes for the flavors to meld and the shallots to soften.

Whisk the olive oil into the shallot mixture and add a few cracks of pepper, if you like. Set aside.

MAKE THE SALAD: In a large cast-iron skillet or heavy sauté pan, heat the olive oil over medium heat. Toss in the bread cubes and toast, frequently shaking the pan, until the bread is golden on all sides, about 4 minutes. Season with a sprinkle of salt and a few cracks of pepper. Transfer the croutons to a large bowl and set aside.

Halve and pit the peaches, then slice into ½-inch wedges. Cut the cucumber in half lengthwise and use a spoon to remove the seeds. Slice the cucumber into ¼-inch half-moons.

Transfer the peaches and cucumbers to the bowl of croutons, add the vinaigrette, and toss to coat. Let sit for 10 minutes to marinate.

Add the blackberries, basil, tarragon, and mint to the bowl and gently toss to combine. Garnish with edible flowers, if desired, and serve.

FRIED SQUASH RINGS
with Pear, Dried Cherry & Feta

When you work countless shifts on the line at a diner, the fryer becomes familiar territory. And it's no secret that a quick dip in hot oil is often the cure-all for coaxing out deep, savory flavor from an ingredient. So when I was wracking my brain for a new way to prepare the winter squash that fills the walk-in starting in the fall, the State Fair and all of its delicious fried goodies came to mind. Sure enough, tempura-fried squash rings are like the little doughnuts we'd buy a bag of every summer. When stuffed with a salad of pear, dried cherries, feta, and arugula, they become the perfect sweet-savory starter or side dish on the holiday table.

FOR THE SQUASH

1 delicata squash (about 1½ pounds)

Extra-virgin olive oil, for drizzling

Kosher salt and freshly ground black pepper

A nutmeg (or a piece of one), for grating

Canola or vegetable oil, for deep-frying

⅔ cup all-purpose flour, plus more for dredging

¾ cup club soda

FOR THE SALAD

2 tablespoons seasoned rice wine vinegar

1 tablespoon finely diced shallots

2 tablespoons extra-virgin olive oil

2 firm but ripe pears, cut into matchsticks

⅓ cup crumbled feta cheese

¼ cup dried cherries

A handful of baby arugula

The nutmeg (from the squash), for grating

¼ cup toasted hazelnuts, roughly chopped (see Cook's Note, page 21)

Maple syrup, for drizzling

COOK'S NOTE: Don't be tempted to overcrowd your oil. Frying more than a few rings of squash at a time will bring down the temperature of the oil, which will cause the squash to get soft and soggy, rather than golden and crispy.

MAKE IT YOUR OWN: Feel free to substitute: Apples for the pears • Golden raisins or dried cranberries for the dried cherries • Grated Parmesan or pecorino for the feta • Walnuts for the hazelnuts

PREHEAT THE OVEN TO 400°F. Line a baking sheet with aluminum foil and set aside.

Make the squash: Cut the squash crosswise into 6 slices, each about 1 inch wide (discard the ends). Remove the seeds with a spoon. Place the rings on the prepared baking sheet, drizzle with olive oil, and season to taste with salt, pepper, and a few grates of nutmeg.

Wrap the squash up in the foil and roast until tender, about 25 minutes. Remove from the oven and let the squash cool to room temperature.

In a deep fryer or large deep skillet, bring a few inches of oil to 375°F. Spread a few tablespoons of flour on a plate in an even layer and set aside. Put the ⅔ cup flour in a medium bowl and slowly add the club soda, whisking until smooth.

Working in batches, dredge the squash rings in the flour, turning to coat, followed by the batter. Fry the squash rings until golden, turning them about halfway through. Transfer the fried squash to a baking sheet lined with paper towels and sprinkle with salt to taste.

MAKE THE SALAD: In a medium bowl, combine the vinegar and shallots and let sit for 10 to 15 minutes for the flavors to meld and the shallots to soften.

Whisk the olive oil into the shallot mixture. Add the pears, feta, and dried cherries and toss to combine.

Arrange the squash rings on a platter and place a few arugula leaves in the center of each one. Divide the pear salad among the rings. Grate some fresh nutmeg over each squash ring, sprinkle them with the chopped hazelnuts, and finish each one with a drizzle of maple syrup. Serve immediately.

ROASTED POTATO SALAD
with Green Beans, Olives & Herbs

SERVES 6

While, yes, this is a salad made from potatoes, the only thing it has in common with the mayo-y BBQ mainstay is the name. It is more of a Mediterranean-style salad of creamy new potatoes that are laced with crisp green beans and salty olives and heaped with a tuft of fresh herbs, which makes for excellent aromatic drama when tossed tableside.

2 tablespoons finely chopped shallots

1 garlic clove, minced

2 tablespoons seasoned rice wine vinegar

1 tablespoon fresh lemon juice

1½ pounds baby potatoes

¾ cup kosher salt

2 handfuls ice cubes

5 ounces green beans, stems removed

½ cup pitted and halved green olives, such as Castelvetrano

¼ cup pitted Niçoise olives

2 tablespoons extra-virgin olive oil

½ cup small fresh basil leaves (purple, if you can find them!)

¼ cup fresh dill

¼ cup fresh flat-leaf parsley leaves

2 tablespoons Brown Butter (page 168), melted

Grated zest of 1 lemon

½ teaspoon Maldon salt

Freshly ground black pepper, for serving

IN A SMALL BOWL, combine the shallots, garlic, vinegar, and lemon juice. Set aside to allow the flavors to meld while you prepare the other ingredients.

In a medium pot, combine the potatoes, ¼ cup of the kosher salt, and just enough water to cover. Bring to a boil over medium-high heat and cook until the potatoes are just tender when pierced with a knife, 25 to 30 minutes. Drain the potatoes and set aside until they're cool enough to handle.

Once they are cooled, halve or quarter the potatoes, depending on their size, and set aside.

Fill a large bowl with the ice and cold water and set aside.

In a large pot, combine 12 cups (3 quarts) water with the remaining ½ cup kosher salt and bring to a rolling boil over medium-high heat. Add the green beans and cook until they are bright green and tender but still crunchy, barely 1 minute. Immediately drain the beans, transfer them to the ice bath, and chill them until cool to the touch, 2 to 3 minutes. Drain the green beans again and slice diagonally into 1½-inch pieces.

In a medium bowl, combine the potatoes, green beans, green olives, and Niçoise olives; add the shallot and garlic mixture and olive oil; and gently toss well to coat. In a small bowl, combine the basil, dill, and parsley.

Spread the potato mixture on a decorative platter and drizzle with the brown butter. Sprinkle with the lemon zest, Maldon salt, and herbs.

To serve, gently toss the salad in front of your guests. Set out a pepper grinder for guests to season their own portions.

SIMPLE IS BEST

SOMETIMES A SALAD DOESN'T HAVE TO BE MUCH MORE THAN . . .

Fresh melon with mint, salt, and lime

Buttered corn with herbs

Boiled potatoes with olive oil and flaky salt

Sliced tomatoes with salt and olive oil
(PHOTO ON PAGES 98–99)

SUMMER SQUASH ROLLS
with Herbed Ricotta & Toasted Hazelnuts

These are sweet little bundles of summer deliciousness. They're sort of a departure from my usual style of throwing a bunch of things onto a plate, but I assure you that there is nothing frilly or fussy here. Thin slices of squash are rolled up with cool, creamy ricotta and mint and basil, plus buttery toasted hazelnuts, for an Italian-inspired bite that guests can pop into their mouths.

1 medium zucchini or summer squash (about 8 ounces)

Extra-virgin olive oil, for coating

Kosher salt and freshly ground black pepper

1 cup fresh ricotta cheese

⅓ cup grated Parmesan cheese, plus a chunk of cheese for shaving

1 tablespoon chopped fresh chives

1 tablespoon chopped fresh dill

Grated zest of 1 lemon

8 fresh basil leaves

8 fresh mint leaves

1 bunch arugula

2 tablespoons Shallot Dressing (page 157)

1 tablespoon hazelnuts, toasted until fragrant and coarsely chopped

PREHEAT THE OVEN TO 425°F.

Use a vegetable peeler or mandoline to slice the squash lengthwise into ¼-inch-thick slices. You want 8 slices total, ideally from the middle of the squash, so your strips will be about 6 inches long.

Arrange the squash ribbons in a single layer on a baking sheet and drizzle each ribbon with just enough olive oil to coat. Season with salt and a few cracks of pepper and roast until tender, about 3 minutes. Set aside to cool completely.

In a medium bowl, combine the ricotta, Parmesan, chives, dill, lemon zest, a good pinch of salt, and a few cracks of pepper.

Stack 1 basil leaf, 1 mint leaf, and 3 arugula leaves crosswise on one end of a squash ribbon. Top with a heaping tablespoon of the ricotta filling, then roll up the slice of squash to create a little bundle and place it seam side down on a platter. Repeat with the remaining squash, herbs, and filling.

Drizzle the rolls with the vinaigrette and sprinkle the crushed hazelnuts over. Use a vegetable peeler to garnish the rolls with wide shavings of Parmesan. Serve immediately.

GREEN BEANS
with Sage, Garlic & Breadcrumbs

Credit for this dish goes to my friend Karen, who hired me to work for her catering company after I had my son, Jaim, and needed a job. I would watch in awe as this petite woman threw around these enormous skillets full of green beans, the aroma of garlic and sage coming off the pans. The dish was, like her, the perfect workhorse—able to pack a ton of flavor with minimal ingredients that didn't need too much coddling and would feed a crowd. I didn't think it was possible to improve on this dish, but then I added buttery homemade breadcrumbs and a hit of lemon zest, and let's just say that you'll be thanking Karen too.

½ cup plus ½ teaspoon kosher salt

12 ounces green beans, stems removed

2 tablespoons extra-virgin olive oil

3 tablespoons Basic Breadcrumbs (page 169)

Grated zest and juice of 1 lemon

2 garlic cloves, chopped

1 tablespoon unsalted butter

2 tablespoons finely chopped fresh sage

Maldon salt

FILL A LARGE BOWL with a couple handfuls of ice and cold water and set aside.

In a large pot, combine 12 cups (3 quarts) water with ½ cup of the kosher salt and bring to a boil over medium-high heat. Add the green beans and blanch just until they are bright green and tender but still crunchy, 30 to 45 seconds. Immediately drain the green beans and transfer them to the ice bath. Allow them to cool for a few minutes, then drain again. Refrigerate them while you prepare the other ingredients.

In a small skillet set over medium heat, swirl 1 tablespoon of the olive oil to coat the bottom of the pan. Add the breadcrumbs and stir to coat them with the oil. Cook, stirring frequently to toast the crumbs evenly, until they are crispy and brown, 3 to 4 minutes. Remove the pan from the heat, stir in the lemon zest, and set aside.

In a large skillet, heat the remaining 1 tablespoon olive oil over high heat. Once it begins to smoke, add the green beans, the remaining ½ teaspoon salt, the garlic, and butter. Cook, tossing the beans frequently to coat, until the butter melts and the garlic begins to brown just a bit, about 1 minute. Add the lemon juice and sage, toss once more, and remove the pan from the heat.

Spread the beans on a serving platter and top with the breadcrumbs and a sprinkle of Maldon salt. Serve immediately.

A SALAD OF LEAVES & BLOOMS

When I was a little girl, one of my favorite bedtime tales was from a 1960s book by English author Molly Brett. It was a story about a group of woodland creatures—hedgehogs, owls, frogs, rabbits—who were looking for a place to build their home. They encountered all sorts of challenges along the way, but once they found the perfect spot, they all croaked and hooted at once: "This is the place for me!" In celebration of their homecoming, they collected treasures from the forest to make a special meal. It was the simplest, most gorgeous salad, made of succulent lettuce leaves dotted with forget-me-nots, and they served their creation on lily pads. Even at a young age, I could understand the magic that could come from such a dish.

To me, the perfect salad is one that looks like it fell from the heavens into a sky-high mound. (I'm always telling the ladies, "Tight and tall!") The leaves should be recognizable as belonging to a head of lettuce (no puny leaves or torn-up lettuce—a salad should be served with a steak knife!) and just misted with vinaigrette. (Don't let your salad drown—unless it's a wedge salad, page 83.) This recipe is sort of like the Universal Salad Standard. As long as you follow these basic guidelines, you're guaranteed to make big, beautiful ones from here on out.

2 teaspoons rice wine vinegar

2 teaspoons finely diced shallots

8 ounces mixed lettuce leaves

1 teaspoon extra-virgin olive oil

Edible flowers, such as nasturtiums, calendula, bachelor's buttons, and/or pansies

Freshly ground black pepper, for serving

IN A SMALL BOWL, combine the vinegar and shallots. Let the mixture marinate for 15 minutes for the flavors to meld and the shallots to soften.

In a chilled stainless steel bowl, using your hands, gently toss the lettuce leaves with the shallot mixture and the olive oil. Be tender with the leaves, so as not to tear or bruise them.

Arrange the leaves in a beautiful bowl or on a platter, sprinkle with edible flowers, and serve with fresh pepper.

COOK'S NOTE: Tossing the leaves in a chilled bowl will help keep your lettuces perky. Always use your hands to toss a salad, and be gentle. Tongs will only damage the leaves. Rinsing your hands in very cold water to chill them down before tossing the lettuces will also help. When plating, think of the leaves of lettuce as being like feathers falling gently from the clouds—they should mound in a nice, high tuft.

CREAMY POLENTA

Pillowy, creamy polenta is the ultimate back-pocket recipe because it comes together in minutes, complements just about any dish, and can be adorned with an endless number of toppings. I love it heaped with roasted mushrooms or a fried egg and herbs, spooned beside slow-cooked meats and their drippings, or served as a surprising warm-weather accompaniment to simply cooked fish.

1½ teaspoons kosher salt

1 cup coarse polenta

⅓ cup grated pecorino cheese

4 tablespoons cold unsalted butter

Freshly ground black pepper

IN A MEDIUM HEAVY-BOTTOMED POT, bring 4 cups water and the salt to a rolling boil over high heat. Slowly whisk in the polenta and continue whisking until you can feel the polenta becoming at home with the water, about 2 minutes. Reduce the heat to low and continue to whisk for another 5 minutes. Then continue cooking, whisking occasionally, until the polenta is creamy and thickened, 10 to 15 minutes.

Remove the pot from the heat, whisk in the cheese and butter, and add pepper to taste. Serve immediately.

COOK'S NOTE: Polenta will thicken as it sits. If you need to make it ahead of time, add a bit of cream and then heat the polenta over low heat to incorporate. Be sure to also adjust the seasoning with more salt, as the cream will soften the flavors. But I assure you that it will come back to life.

ROSEMARY FRENCH FRITES

Homemade French fries will always merit the time and energy required because not only can you achieve that crispy outside–soft inside golden ratio, but you can also eat them as intended—within seconds of coming out of the fryer. Plus, show me a drive-thru that sprinkles their fries with fresh garlic and rosemary. Add a basket of these to a meal, and there's not a person at the table who won't get the heartfelt message: *You're worth it*.

2 pounds Yukon Gold potatoes, peeled

Neutral oil, for deep-frying

1 large garlic clove, minced

1 teaspoon extra-virgin olive oil

Kosher salt

2 tablespoons finely chopped fresh rosemary

Garlicky Mayonnaise (page 164), for serving (optional)

FILL A LARGE BOWL with cold water. Using a mandoline with the large-tooth blade, or a very sharp knife, slice the potatoes into French fry–sized pieces and submerge them in the water. Cover and refrigerate the sliced potatoes overnight to release the starch, draining and replacing the water after about the first 4 hours.

In a deep fryer or large deep skillet, bring a few inches of oil to 325°F.

Drain the potatoes in a colander and give them a good shake—water is not a friend of hot oil! Fry the potatoes in batches until just cooked through but not at all brown, 4 to 5 minutes. Transfer the fries to a large, clean bowl. If you plan on serving the frites later, refrigerate the potatoes until you're ready to finish and serve them; otherwise, carry on.

In a small bowl, combine the garlic, olive oil, and a good pinch of salt. Set aside.

Bring the oil temperature up to 375°F, if it's not already. Working in batches, re-fry the potatoes until golden brown, shaking the basket or stirring with a kitchen spider or slotted spoon now and again to keep the frites from sticking together, 2 to 3 minutes. As with any frying, avoid overcrowding, to ensure a crispy result.

Transfer the fries to a large bowl and immediately toss with the garlic mixture and rosemary. Season with a good amount of salt and serve immediately, if you like, with the garlic mayo.

HONEYED BEETS
with Feta & Toasted Pistachios

Beets can be divisive, I know. You either love them or you . . . do not. But the trick is to lean into their natural sweetness and use bright, acidic flavors to balance their earthiness. This recipe takes a page from Greek flavor combinations, using honey and feta to tame those beets with an assist from citrus and a sprinkling of sweet-salty nuts. Serve this with a roasted chicken (or with last night's roasted chicken for a really nice salad), black bass, or any thin crispy white fish.

2 tablespoons thinly sliced shallots

2 tablespoons seasoned rice wine vinegar

1½ pounds red or golden beets, root and stems trimmed (I like leaving about an inch of the stems because it's a nice, and beautiful, reminder that these came from the ground)

½ cup kosher salt

1 tablespoon extra-virgin olive oil

Juice of 1 lime

2½ ounces feta cheese (I'm happy with either sheep's- or cow's-milk feta), crumbled

1 tablespoon honey

3 tablespoons pistachios, toasted until fragrant and coarsely chopped

¼ cup loosely packed fresh mint leaves

IN A SMALL BOWL, combine the shallots and vinegar. Set aside to let the flavors meld and the shallots soften while you prepare the beets.

In a small pot, combine the beets and salt and add just enough water to cover. Bring to a boil over medium-high heat and cook until the beets are tender but still very firm when pierced with a knife, about 45 minutes. Drain the beets in a colander and run under cold water to stop the cooking process. Set aside.

When the beets are cool enough to handle, use your hands to slip off the skins. Quarter the beets lengthwise into 1-inch wedges, or, if they are larger, feel free to slice them into smaller pieces.

In a medium bowl, toss the beets with the shallots and vinegar and set aside to marinate for at least 20 minutes, or up to 1 hour.

Using a slotted spoon, transfer the beets to a decorative platter and arrange them in a single layer. Drizzle with the olive oil and lime juice. Tuck the feta in among the beets, drizzle everything with the honey, and sprinkle with the toasted nuts. Dot with the mint leaves and serve immediately.

CRISPY CAULIFLOWER
with Honey & Hot Pepper Flakes

This dish came together on a whim. Five o' clock was rapidly approaching, and with it, a dining room full of hungry guests. But I had resolved to put a new side dish on that evening's menu. Well, when under pressure, we can surprise ourselves with what we can accomplish, and what started as a freaked-out throw-together became a delicious discovery. Crunchy, creamy cauliflower drizzled with a bit of honey and finished with hot pepper flakes is a welcome surprise of flavor—not unlike crispy hot honey chicken.

1 medium head cauliflower, cored and cut into 2-inch florets

1 tablespoon extra-virgin olive oil

Kosher salt and freshly ground black pepper

1½ cups club soda

1 cup all-purpose flour, plus more for dusting

Neutral oil, for deep-frying

2 tablespoons honey

1½ teaspoons chile flakes

Grated zest of ½ lemon

Maldon salt

PREHEAT THE OVEN TO 450°F.

In a large bowl, toss the cauliflower with the olive oil and salt and pepper to taste. Spread the cauliflower out on a baking sheet and roast until crisp-tender, about 5 minutes. Set aside to cool.

In a medium bowl, whisk together the club soda and flour; set aside.

In a deep fryer or large, deep skillet, bring a few inches of oil to 375°F.

In a large bowl, lightly toss the roasted cauliflower in flour, then, working in batches, dredge the florets in the batter and fry until golden, 2 to 3 minutes. Be careful not to overcrowd the oil, or the florets will lower the temperature of the oil and become soggy.

Transfer the hot fried cauliflower to a platter; drizzle with the honey; and sprinkle with the chile flakes, lemon zest, and a few generous pinches of Maldon salt. Eat straightaway and hot!

COOK'S NOTE: This is the party-sized version of this recipe; it can be halved for a smaller gathering or family meal.

PERFECT POTATO PUREE
with Bay Leaf & Thyme

A heaping bowl of fluffy mashed spuds was almost always at the center of my grandparents' dinner table. My grandmother could be counted on to add yet another pat of butter to my serving before I swabbed it all up with her perfectly roasted chicken or crusty bits of steak. I wanted to offer my own spin on this dish, so I infused the cream with bay leaf and thyme. The effect is rich, creamy mashed potatoes worthy of my childhood memories, but with even more depth of flavor. Believe me when I tell you that whenever this is on the menu at the restaurant, I always factor in a bowlful—or two—for myself.

FOR THE INFUSED CREAM

½ cup heavy cream

4 sprigs fresh thyme

2 dried bay leaves

FOR THE MASHED POTATOES

3 pounds potatoes (such as russet or Yukon Gold), peeled and cubed

4 garlic cloves, peeled

2 heaping tablespoons kosher salt, or more to taste

12 tablespoons (1½ sticks) unsalted butter

Freshly ground black pepper

COOK'S NOTE: A food mill is highly recommended for this recipe because of the smooth texture you can achieve with it without overworking the potatoes (which can make them gluey). I promise you won't regret the modest investment; it's the gateway to many more silky purees to come.

You can easily make this puree a day or two in advance of serving and reheat to serve. It will taste just as rich and delicious, without all the running around the day of. For an even creamier, more velvety consistency, pass the pureed potatoes through a chinois (super-fine mesh sieve). It's a bit of work and time—and most likely best left for occasions when you want to impress—but wow, will it take your spuds to a sexy new level.

MAKE IT YOUR OWN: You can change the flavor of the potato puree by changing up what you steep in the cream. Here are a few suggestions:

• Fresh rosemary or sage

• Toasted spices, such as fennel or coriander seeds or juniper berries

MAKE THE INFUSED CREAM: In a small saucepan, bring the cream, thyme, and bay leaves to a slow simmer over medium heat. Turn off the heat and let the cream steep for at least 20 minutes.

Strain the cream into a medium bowl and set aside.

MAKE THE POTATOES: In a large pot, combine the potatoes, garlic, salt, and enough water to cover and bring to a boil over medium-high heat. Reduce the heat to a simmer and cook until the potatoes are fork-tender, about 15 minutes. Drain the potatoes (set the pot aside).

Working over a large bowl, in batches, if necessary, push the potatoes and garlic through a food mill fitted with the finest screen.

Add the milled potatoes back to the pot and set over low heat. Stir in the butter, followed by half of the steeped cream. Then stir in a bit more of the cream, and keep adding all of it until the potatoes just barely hold a peak when you lift the spoon. Taste for salt and add a few good cracks of pepper. Serve immediately.

SUPPERS

TO SATISFY, TO PROVIDE, TO SAVOR

———

Seared Tuna
with Summer Fruit & Cucumber 119

Lavender-&-Juniper-Crusted Lamb 120

Fennel Fried Chicken & Backyard Biscuits
with Strawberry-Rhubarb Sweet and Sour 125

Buttered Cod with Fennel, Olives,
Capers & Croutons 130

A Skillet of Scallops
with Cedar, Chorizo & Lime 133

Garlicky Mignon Steaks
with Caramelized Onion Butter 137

Wednesday Night Fish Fry 138

Brown-Sugar–&-Maple-Glazed Pork Tenderloin
with Roasted Fruit 140

Pickle-Brined Roasted Chicken 145

A Farmhouse Pie with Duck Confit,
Roasted Grapes & Shallots 146

Duck Confit 149

Skillet Cutlets
with Fennel Pollen & Mustard 151

The main course is *the* moment. It's the reason why everyone's showing up, truly. *Come for supper. What's for dinner?* The appetizers, the salad, the soup—that's all just building anticipation for the one plate that's going to define the evening. With that comes a lot of pressure. You want to meet people's expectations of a dish that's going to fill their bellies *and* that feels special. But, at the same time, a plate heaped high with "fancy" ingredients can fall short—which is why, instead of getting hung up on the idea of impressing people, I like to think of this course as an opportunity to deeply satisfy them. A thoughtful main dish has the ability to slow time, inviting your guests to linger a little longer and sink into the here and now.

When I'm planning a meal, I always start with the main course, because I want it to be the centerpiece that everything else supports. First I think about my protein, because it is the center of that center, so it needs to be the best I can find—a gorgeous well-raised steak, the freshest fish at the market, a beautiful chicken tended to by a local farmer. From there, I layer. I close my eyes and think about how I'll be using my fork to build bites, with textures and flavors that marry well. It's that conversation between the ingredients—the salty, the creamy, the bright, the rich, the sweet, the crunchy—that becomes complex, not the preparations themselves. Any of these dishes would make a special meal in its own right. Whether you're cooking by season, by protein, or by preference, don't worry; I have you covered.

SEARED TUNA
with Summer Fruit & Cucumber

This is the ultimate warm-weather dish. It's quick-cooking, so your time in a hot kitchen is short. And, if you like, you can make the tuna ahead and slice and serve it as a chilled lunch or dinner. And then, of course, there's the combination of succulent, juicy nectarines and melon with crisp, cool cucumber and naturally sweet tuna. It's basically summer on a plate.

Grated zest and juice of 1 lime, plus lime wedges for garnish

1 tablespoon seasoned rice wine vinegar

2 nectarines, halved, pitted, and cut into ½-inch slices (see Cook's Note)

1 medium cucumber, cut into ⅓-inch slices (see Cook's Note)

½ cup cantaloupe cut into organically shaped 1-inch pieces

1 heaping tablespoon small to medium fresh Thai basil leaves

1 heaping tablespoon small to medium fresh mint leaves

1 heaping tablespoon fresh tarragon leaves

1 heaping tablespoon chopped fresh dill

2 tablespoons extra-virgin olive oil

4 (6-ounce) tuna steaks (1 inch thick)

Kosher salt and freshly ground black pepper

Edible flowers, for garnish (optional)

IN A MEDIUM BOWL, combine the lime zest and juice with the vinegar. Let the mixture sit for 15 minutes to marry the flavors.

Add the nectarines, cucumber, and cantaloupe to the bowl and gently toss to coat. Add the basil, mint, tarragon, and dill and gently toss again to combine. Set aside.

In a large cast-iron skillet or heavy sauté pan, heat the oil over high heat. Season the tuna with salt and pepper. When the oil begins to smoke, carefully add the tuna steaks to the pan. Sear the fish until it is nice and brown on the first side, about 2 minutes. Flip and cook for 2 more minutes, or until the second side is browned. Remove from the heat and transfer the tuna to a platter. You can serve the fish now, or transfer it to the refrigerator to chill for at least 1 hour, or up to overnight.

If serving the fish warm, arrange the fruit salad over the fish and serve immediately, with lime wedges and a scattering of edible flowers, if desired. If serving chilled, slice the tuna into 1-inch-wide pieces, arrange them on plates, then top with the salad, lime wedges, and (optional) flowers.

COOK'S NOTE: No need to peel or seed the cucumber as long as the flesh is tender. Keep the skin on the nectarines for added color.

LAVENDER-&-JUNIPER-CRUSTED LAMB

Rack of lamb is the queen of impressive dishes, but this one in particular? We're talking ruler of rulers. I've pulled out all the stops with a crust for some crunch, plus a sticky-sweet honey-orange glaze that gets studded with lavender, juniper, and pistachio—a combination that blends seamlessly into a perfectly balanced medley and cuts the richness of the meat. But the best part is that it takes virtually no time to come together and goes oven-to-table in under an hour. Plus, you can serve this as an entrée or as an appetizer. Just be forewarned: your friends may ask, "Why don't you open a restaurant?"

2 large garlic cloves, minced

2 tablespoons rosewater

1 (2½-pound) rack of lamb with 8 rib bones, preferably Frenched (you can ask your butcher to do this if necessary)

Kosher salt and freshly ground black pepper

2 tablespoons extra-virgin olive oil, plus more as needed

2 tablespoons Dijon mustard

2 tablespoons honey

1 tablespoon grated orange zest

1 heaping teaspoon juniper berries

½ cup roasted and chopped pistachios

2 teaspoons dried lavender flowers

1 tablespoon chopped fresh rosemary

⅓ cup panko breadcrumbs

IN A SMALL BOWL, marinate the garlic in the rosewater for at least 20 minutes.

Preheat the oven to 350°F. Set a cooling rack on a baking sheet and set aside.

Season the lamb with 1 tablespoon salt and 1 teaspoon pepper. Set a large skillet over medium heat, add a bit of olive oil, and heat it until hot, then brown the lamb on all sides, about 2 minutes per side. Set the lamb aside until it's cool enough to handle.

Drain off and discard the rosewater, leaving the garlic in the bowl. Add the mustard, honey, and orange zest and whisk to combine. Brush the mixture evenly over the lamb. If your rack is Frenched (meaning the fat and meat have been removed from the rib bones), you do not need to coat the rib bones. If it is not "Frenched," feel free to coat the entire rack.

COOK'S NOTE: If you prefer your lamb more on the medium side, cook for an additional 5 or so minutes, until the internal temperature is 130 to 135°F.

In the bowl of a food processor, pulse the juniper berries until finely ground. Add the pistachios and pulse 15 times, or until they are coarsely ground. Add the dried lavender and pulse 15 more times, or until finely ground but not quite dust.

Transfer the juniper mixture to a medium bowl and add the panko and salt and pepper to taste. Stir to combine.

Coat the lamb with the panko mixture, pressing gently to make sure it sticks. Set the lamb on the rack on the baking sheet and roast for 25 to 30 minutes, until the internal thermometer reaches 125 to 130°F for rare to medium-rare. Remove from the oven, cover the roasted lamb with foil, and let it rest for 10 minutes.

With a carving knife, cut between the ribs to create individual chops. Arrange the chops on a platter and serve immediately.

FENNEL FRIED CHICKEN & BACKYARD BISCUITS
with Strawberry-Rhubarb Sweet and Sour

Fried chicken has been a staple on my menu ever since I started feeding people for a living. To my mind, it doesn't get more nostalgic or satisfying. There are some things I'll never mess with when it comes to the time-tested recipe, such as brining the meat to flavor it from the inside out and dredging it in cornflakes (the least fancy you can find). But I like to have a little fun too by introducing unexpected flavors. One of my favorite additions is fennel, which I include in the brine for its barely there sweetness, plus a sprinkling of fennel pollen when the chicken is fresh out of the fryer. Then I serve the perfectly crispy, salty chicken with a sweet-tart sauce. Whether you offer this up hot out of the pan or cold and packed up for lunch, this version's going to be your new go-to crowd pleaser.

FOR THE STRAWBERRY-RHUBARB SWEET AND SOUR

2 cups rhubarb cut into ½-inch pieces

½ cup granulated sugar

1 cup hulled strawberries chopped into ½-inch pieces

3 tablespoons cider vinegar

Freshly ground black pepper

FOR THE FRIED CHICKEN

⅓ cup granulated sugar

⅓ cup kosher salt

4 dried bay leaves

2 tablespoons fennel seeds

1 tablespoon black peppercorns

1 (3- to 4-pound) chicken, cut into 10 pieces

4 cups all-purpose flour

4 cups cornflakes

2 tablespoons cornstarch

Neutral oil, such as canola or vegetable, for deep-frying

1 tablespoon ground fennel

2 cups buttermilk (well shaken before measuring)

1 tablespoon Maldon salt

2 teaspoons fennel pollen

Nasturtium flowers, for garnish (optional)

Backyard Biscuits (recipe follows)

-recipe continues-

COOK'S NOTE: The chicken will need to brine overnight, so be sure to leave yourself enough time. If your biscuits aren't piping hot by the time your chicken is done, no big deal! Even warm biscuits would be perfect. Just don't serve them cold; see page 127 for reheating instructions.

MAKE THE SWEET AND SOUR: In a medium heavy-bottomed saucepan, combine the rhubarb and sugar and bring to a simmer over medium heat, stirring frequently, until the rhubarb breaks down and becomes tender and saucy, about 5 minutes. Remove the pan from the heat and stir in the strawberries, vinegar, and a few cracks of pepper. Let cool completely. (This will keep in an airtight jar or container in the fridge for up to 1 week.)

MAKE THE CHICKEN: In a large pot, combine the sugar, kosher salt, bay leaves, fennel seeds, and peppercorns with 4 cups water. Bring the mixture to a boil over high heat, stirring until the salt and sugar dissolve. Remove the pot from the heat and let the brine cool completely before using. (It will keep in the fridge for up to 2 weeks.)

Once the brine is completely cool, add the chicken pieces, cover the pot, and refrigerate overnight.

The next day, set the pot over medium heat and bring the brine to a simmer. Cook until the chicken is no longer pink inside (I take a little peek with a knife), about 20 minutes. Use tongs to transfer the chicken to a plate and let cool. Discard the brine.

In a gallon-sized zip-top bag, combine 2 cups of the flour, the cornflakes, and cornstarch. Seal the bag and use your hands to crush the cornflakes and thoroughly combine the mixture.

In a deep fryer or large deep skillet, bring a few inches of oil to 375°F. Line a baking sheet or large plate with paper towels and set aside.

In a shallow baking dish, whisk together the remaining 2 cups flour and the ground fennel. Pour the buttermilk into a second shallow dish. Put the cornflake mixture in a third shallow dish.

Dredge each piece of the chicken in the flour and fennel mixture, then the buttermilk, and then the cornflake mixture. Place the dredged chicken on a plate. Working in batches, drop the coated chicken pieces into the oil and fry, turning as needed, until evenly golden brown, 5 to 6 minutes. Take care not to overcrowd the oil, or the temperature will drop, causing your chicken to become greasy instead of nice and crisp. Transfer the chicken to the paper towel–lined baking sheet or plate and immediately sprinkle with the Maldon salt and fennel pollen.

Serve the chicken with the biscuits and strawberry-rhubarb sweet and sour. Garnish with nasturtium blooms, if you'd like.

Backyard Biscuits

During the summer of 2020, when we had to completely rethink the way we cared for our guests, my team of strong, resilient women immediately got to work turning the backyard into an outdoor dining space, and when it came to the menu, I resolved to serve the kind of food that had the power to reassure people that everything was going to be OK. My mind immediately went to these biscuits, which bring me back to my childhood and memories of my beloved grandfather and his delicious cooking.

3¼ cups all-purpose flour,
plus more for sprinkling

1 cup (2 sticks) unsalted butter, cubed

2½ teaspoons baking powder

2 teaspoons kosher salt

2 teaspoons granulated sugar

¼ teaspoon baking soda

1 cup buttermilk (well shaken
before measuring)

Melted unsalted butter, for brushing

Maldon salt, for sprinkling

IN THE BOWL OF a food processor, combine the flour, butter, baking powder, kosher salt, sugar, and baking soda and pulse until small, pea-sized beads form.

Transfer the mixture to a medium bowl. Slowly add the buttermilk, mixing with a wooden spoon as you pour. The dough will be quite dry, but don't let it trick you into overworking it. Turn the dough out onto a floured surface and roll into a 6 x 12-inch rectangle. Cut the dough lengthwise into 3 rectangles and stack them on top of each other. Roll out the stack again into a 6 x 12-inch rectangle, cut the dough into 3 rectangles, and stack again. Roll out the dough to a 1-inch thickness.

Line a baking sheet with parchment paper. Using a round 3-inch biscuit cutter, cut out 6 biscuits (discard the dough scraps). Place the biscuits on the prepared baking sheet 2 inches apart. Freeze the biscuits for 15 minutes.

Preheat the oven to 425°F.

Brush the tops of the biscuits with melted butter and sprinkle with a little Maldon salt. Bake until the biscuits are golden and just cooked through, 12 to 15 minutes.

Serve hot and fresh out of the oven. Store any leftovers in an airtight container at room temperature for up to 3 days. To reheat, slice the biscuits in half and toast, or spread them with a bit of butter and griddle them in a skillet.

COOK'S NOTE: One way to guarantee those buttery layers is to "Resist the Twist." Push the biscuit cutter down into the dough so that you don't seal the biscuits and prohibit the layers from separating as they bake. Also, cut out the biscuits as economically as you can. These scraps cannot be rerolled because the dough will become tough, and you won't get those flaky layers.

BUTTERED COD
with Fennel, Olives, Capers & Croutons

The beauty of this mild, juicy, flaky fish is that it's easy to cook well at home (the secret is in the butter), and you can complement it with any number of flavors. I love layering it with salty olives and capers, the fresh crunch of fennel, and warm croutons—it's like you've gone to Italy for a moment. You don't need anything else on your plate for a perfectly satisfying meal.

2 tablespoons finely chopped shallots

2 tablespoons seasoned rice wine vinegar

¼ cup plus 1 tablespoon extra-virgin olive oil

2 cups cubed crusty bread (I like ½-inch cubes)

1 fennel bulb, halved, cored, and very thinly sliced, fronds reserved for garnish (if you like)

½ cup halved and pitted green olives, such as Castelvetrano

1 tablespoon capers (I like brine-packed), drained

2 teaspoons chopped fresh chives

1 teaspoon chopped fresh dill

Grated zest and juice of 1 small lemon

4 (5- to 6-ounce) cod fillets, skin left on

Kosher salt and freshly ground black pepper (optional)

6 tablespoons unsalted butter

IN A MEDIUM BOWL, combine the shallots and vinegar. Set the mixture aside for 15 minutes to allow the flavors to meld and the shallots to soften.

Preheat the oven to 425°F.

In a large cast-iron skillet or heavy sauté pan, heat 2 tablespoons of the oil over medium heat. Add the bread cubes and cook, stirring frequently, until toasted, 3 to 4 minutes. Remove the pan from the heat.

In a large bowl, combine the bread with the shallot and vinegar mixture, fennel, olives, capers, chives, dill, and lemon zest and toss gently to coat. Set aside while you cook the fish.

Pat each cod fillet dry with paper towels to remove any surface moisture. This will help you get a good, crispy sear. Generously season both sides of each fillet with salt, and pepper if you like.

In a large cast-iron skillet or heavy ovenproof sauté pan, heat the remaining 3 tablespoons oil over high heat until smoking. Gently add the fish fillets skin side

-recipe continues-

COOK'S NOTE: A cherry pitter works wonders for getting stubborn pits out of olives. Alternatively, a good smash with the side of a chef's knife will do the trick as well.

down and cook until golden, 2 to 3 minutes. Flip the fish and cook for another 30 seconds, then add the butter, swirling the pan to help it melt.

Transfer the skillet to the oven and roast the fish until it's flaky and cooked through, 4 to 5 minutes.

Transfer the bread salad to a serving platter. Baste the fish with the pan juices and nestle the fillets over the salad. Drizzle a bit of the buttery pan juices over the top, along with the lemon juice. Garnish with the fennel fronds, if you like, and serve.

A SKILLET OF SCALLOPS
with Cedar, Chorizo & Lime

The magic of this dish begins with how wildly easy it is to make and ends with how impressive it is to guests. Foraged cedar makes for an unexpected twist and lends both warmth and unparalleled flavor to a simple skillet of juicy scallops bathed in a smoky chorizo butter, with hints of the woods. Serve this family-style right from the skillet.

To serve this as an appetizer, set out the scallops with good bread, grilled with olive oil and rubbed with garlic.

1 pound large (U-10) scallops
(about 12)

Kosher salt and freshly ground
black pepper

2 tablespoons extra-virgin olive oil

1 packed cup fresh cedar sprigs
(see Cook's Note)

4 tablespoons unsalted butter

⅓ cup diced Spanish chorizo,
chopped into raisin-sized bits

1 lime, halved

REMOVE THE "FEET" FROM the scallops if your fishmonger hasn't already (these are the little tough bits on the sides of the scallops). Blot the scallops dry with a paper towel. The more moisture you can remove from the surface, the better the sear will be. Season with a bit of salt and pepper, keeping in mind that scallops can be naturally salty—so consider being a little more conservative with the salt than usual.

In a medium skillet, heat a good drizzle of olive oil over high heat. When the oil begins to smoke, carefully place the scallops in the skillet and sear undisturbed for 2 to 3 minutes, until the undersides are nicely browned. Using a pair of tongs, turn the scallops, then add half of the cedar sprigs and cook undisturbed for another minute. Add the butter to the pan, followed by the chorizo. The butter will smoke and make a delicious scene. Once the butter has completely melted, remove the pan from the heat and add the remaining cedar sprigs. Squeeze the lime over the scallops and serve immediately.

COOK'S NOTE: Using foraged ingredients always adds interest to a dish, but if running out into the woods to find cedar sprigs is wildly improbable, rosemary makes a lovely substitution here.

MAKE IT YOUR OWN: You could also try fir tips in the spring, or lavender in the summer, or bits of balsam around the holidays.

GARLICKY MIGNON STEAKS
with Caramelized Onion Butter

Cooking an expensive piece of meat used to stress me out *big time*. The last thing you want to do is spend all of that time, energy, and money, only to mess it all up—and in front of your guests, for all to see. No pressure, right? But I want you to take a nice, deep breath because I'm going to get you through it. Consider this your new no-fail method for preparing beef tenderloin steaks. I'd like to think that all those botched steaks (and no shortage of tears) were well worth it, because this recipe is spot-on.

4 large garlic cloves, peeled

2 teaspoons chopped fresh rosemary

1 tablespoon kosher salt

1 teaspoon onion powder

Freshly ground black pepper

2 tablespoons extra-virgin olive oil, plus more as needed

4 (6-ounce) beef tenderloin steaks (about 1¾ inches thick)

¼ cup Caramelized Onion Butter (page 167)

Edible flowers (I like nasturtiums, calendula, or onion blossoms for this one), for garnish (optional)

USING A MORTAR AND PESTLE, mash the garlic and rosemary with the salt. Add the onion powder, a few twists of pepper, and the olive oil, stirring and mashing with the pestle as you go.

Rub the paste evenly over the steaks, top, bottom, and sides. Put the steaks on a plate, cover with plastic wrap, and refrigerate for at least 6 hours, or up to overnight.

Remove the steaks from the fridge and let them come to room temperature, about 1 hour.

Preheat the oven to 375°F.

Set a medium cast-iron skillet over high heat and drizzle in a bit of olive oil. Brush the rub off the steaks (little bits left behind are fine) and add them to the hot pan. Sear undisturbed so they can form a nice crust on the first side, about 4 minutes. Flip the steaks and cook on the second side for 2 minutes. Transfer the skillet to the oven and roast for 1 minute. Flip the steaks and roast for another minute, for rare. For medium-rare, roast for 2 minutes.

Transfer the hot steaks to a plate, tent with foil, and let them rest for 8 to 10 minutes.

Top each steak with a dollop of the caramelized onion butter, garnish with edible flowers, if using, and serve.

COOK'S NOTE: Cooking meat over a wood fire is always more delicious. Feel free to take it outside!

WEDNESDAY NIGHT FISH FRY

When I first started working at my family's diner as a young girl, I spent most of the time cleaning up after my dad as he bounced from griddle to stovetop, pumping out meal after meal at our busy roadside restaurant. Then, when the time came for me to try my hand at cooking, the first task he awarded me with was frying fish for the diner's signature Wednesday Night Fish Fry. You could say my culinary career was born in the fryolator that day. And, yes, I now know a thing or two about making expertly fried fish. Or, as I like to think of it, the fried fish that all fish dream they'll grow up to be.

¾ cup all-purpose flour

¼ cup plus 2 tablespoons cornstarch

½ teaspoon paprika

1 cup beer, such as lager or golden ale

Neutral oil, for deep-frying

2 pounds thick flaky white fish fillets, such as cod or hake, cut into 1 x 4-inch "fingers"

Kosher salt and freshly ground black pepper

IN A SHALLOW BOWL, whisk together ¼ cup of the flour, 2 tablespoons of the cornstarch, and the paprika. In another shallow bowl, whisk together the remaining ½ cup flour and ¼ cup cornstarch. Add the beer to the second bowl and whisk until the batter is smooth.

In a deep fryer or large, deep skillet, bring a few inches of oil to 375°F. Line a baking sheet with paper towels and set near your frying station.

Season the fish fingers with salt and pepper. Working in batches, dredge the fish in the flour mix, followed by the beer batter. Gently drop the battered fish into the hot oil and fry, turning as needed, until golden brown, 4 to 5 minutes. Transfer the fried fish to the prepared baking sheet to drain, and season with more salt and pepper, if you like.

Serve fresh and hot!

COOK'S NOTE: For a full-on dinner, make a batch of frites (page 107) to go alongside... and some coleslaw and tartar sauce! For extra credit, serve the fish in newspaper cones (see page 270).

BROWN-SUGAR-&-MAPLE-GLAZED PORK TENDERLOIN
with Roasted Fruit

This is my favorite kind of dish: effortless enough for a Monday, but elegant enough for a Saturday. Starting with a spice rub and finishing with a sugary glaze transforms an otherwise straightforward cut of meat into lacquered, tender perfection. I like serving it with a moody side of anise-scented roasted winter fruit such as pears and plums.

FOR THE TENDERLOIN

1 tablespoon ground fennel

2½ teaspoons kosher salt

1 teaspoon freshly ground black pepper

1 teaspoon chili powder

¼ teaspoon ground cinnamon

1 (1¼- to 1½-pound) pork tenderloin

2 teaspoons extra-virgin olive oil

3 whole star anise pods

½ cup packed light brown sugar

½ cup maple syrup

2 garlic cloves, minced

FOR THE ROASTED FRUIT

2 medium pears, halved, cored, and cut into ½-inch slices

1 medium shallot, cut into ¼-inch slices

2 tablespoons plus 1 teaspoon sugar

3 sprigs fresh thyme

Grated zest and juice of 1 medium lemon

5 whole star anise pods

Kosher salt and freshly ground black pepper

2 plums, halved, pitted, and cut into ½-inch slices

MAKE THE TENDERLOIN: In a small bowl, combine the fennel, salt, pepper, chili powder, and cinnamon. Pat the spice mix all over the tenderloin.

In a large, heavy-bottomed skillet, heat the olive oil over medium heat. Add the tenderloin and sear on all sides until browned, about 1½ minutes per side. Transfer the pork to a baking dish and set aside.

In a small saucepan, toast the star anise over medium heat to allow the flavor to open up, about 1 minute. Add the brown sugar, maple syrup, and garlic, stir to combine, and cook until the sugar melts and the glaze begins to bubble, 4 to 5 minutes. Remove the pan from the heat and let sit for 1 hour to let the glaze thicken and the flavors meld.

Preheat the oven to 375°F.

Brush the tenderloin evenly all over with about one third of the glaze. Bake the tenderloin, basting it every 5 minutes or so with more of the glaze, for 15 to 20 minutes, until an instant-read thermometer inserted in the center reaches 160°F.

Transfer the tenderloin to a carving board and tent with foil (do not clean the pan or discard any of the glaze). Let the meat rest while you roast the fruit. Increase the oven temperature to 425°F.

MAKE THE FRUIT: In a medium bowl, toss together the pears with the shallot, 2 tablespoons of the sugar, the thyme, lemon zest, star anise, a good pinch of salt, and a crack of pepper. Spread the mixture over the bottom of a rimmed baking sheet and roast until the pears are just tender, 8 to 10 minutes. Add the plums and lemon juice, toss, and roast for 1 minute more.

Cut the pork into 1-inch-thick medallions and arrange them on a platter with the fruit. Drizzle with a couple spoonfuls of any glaze left in the saucepan and serve.

PICKLE-BRINED ROASTED CHICKEN

This recipe is the marriage of two of my favorite foods: roasted chicken and pickles. I've always brined chicken before roasting it—one of the secrets to juicy, flavored-from-the-inside meat—so I updated my staple recipe to include pickling spices such as coriander, allspice, and dill seeds. Then, I roast the bird stuffed with fresh dill, garlic, and onions—yet another ode to those beloved summer pickles.

1 cup kosher salt

1 cup granulated sugar

½ cup pickling spice (see Cook's Note)

1 whole chicken (about 5 pounds)

2 yellow or white onions, peeled and quartered

1 garlic head, halved horizontally

1 bunch dill flowers, if you can find them (if not, 1 bunch fresh dill)

IN A LARGE POT, combine 12 cups (3 quarts) water, the salt, sugar, and pickling spice and bring to a rolling boil over high heat. Remove the pot from the heat and let the brine cool completely.

Add the chicken to the brine, cover, and refrigerate overnight, or for as long as 24 hours.

Remove the chicken from the brine (discard the brine) and pat it dry with paper towels or a clean kitchen towel. Set the chicken on a cooling rack placed on a baking sheet and refrigerate for 1 hour to air dry.

Remove the chicken from the fridge and let it come to room temperature, about 1 hour. Preheat the oven to 375°F.

Place 4 of the onion quarters in a circle in the center of a roasting pan for the chicken to rest on. Pat the chicken dry again and stuff the cavity with the remaining onion quarters, the halved garlic head, and the dill. Set the chicken on top of the onion quarters. Roast until the chicken juices run clear when a thigh is pierced with a knife, about 1 hour.

Remove the chicken from the oven, tent with foil, and let rest for 10 minutes before carving.

COOK'S NOTE: Splurge on a good-quality chicken, ideally one from a local farmer or a supermarket bird that's been allowed to live most of its life outside eating what a chicken is meant to eat. It might be more expensive, but meat should be a treat, and you will taste the difference.

MAKE IT YOUR OWN: Roast meats, especially roast chicken and especially in the cooler months, pair nicely with roasted fruit. It's an unexpected but delicious edible garnish that's easy to prepare: Toss wedges of pears, apples, or quince with a good drizzle of olive oil and sprinkle with salt and pepper. Roast at 400°F until lightly browned but still tender, about 20 minutes. Immediately add about 1 tablespoon of unsalted butter and toss to coat until glistening.

A FARMHOUSE PIE
with Duck Confit, Roasted Grapes & Shallots

I will admit, there was a lot of debate among all of us at The Lost Kitchen over this recipe. I had no idea that the traditional combination of meat and mashed potatoes baked together in a skillet would mean different things to each of us—and with strong opinions to match. "It's called cottage pie!" "No! It's shepherd's pie!" "It MUST have peas!" "No! It must have corn!" "With lamb!" "No, with beef!" So you can imagine the minor outrage when I suggested that we do it instead not only with duck confit, but also with grapes. The skepticism was palpable, but I could almost taste the succulent duck, creamy potatoes, and deeply sweet bursts of the roast grapes, and I knew that it would be a winning combination. The silence that followed the first bites confirmed my suspicions: This "pie"—no matter what any of us would call it—had hushed all the naysayers.

Extra-virgin olive oil, as needed

2 cups shallots sliced into ¼-inch rings
(about 8 medium shallots)

Kosher salt and freshly ground
black pepper

1 tablespoon unsalted butter

2 cups halved red grapes

2 garlic cloves, finely chopped

1 tablespoon fresh thyme leaves

Grated zest of 1 navel orange

Perfect Potato Puree (page 112)

3 Duck Confit legs (page 149),
meat removed and shredded

ADD ENOUGH OLIVE OIL to a medium skillet to coat the bottom of the pan and heat over low heat. Add the shallots and season to taste with salt and pepper. Cook, stirring occasionally, until the shallots begin to caramelize, about 10 minutes.

Add the butter and cook for just a few minutes, allowing the butter to foam and the color of the shallots to deepen. Transfer the shallots to a small bowl and set aside.

Heat the same pan over high heat until nearly smoking. Add the grapes, garlic, and 2 teaspoons of the thyme. Give the pan a good shake, season the grapes with salt and pepper, shake the pan again, and shut off the heat. Let the grapes sit undisturbed for a few

-recipe continues-

COOK'S NOTE: If you don't have time to make duck confit, store-bought is always a great option. Alternatively, leftover roast chicken or short ribs (or any shredded meat, really) will work if that's what you've got!

minutes while the pan cools down, then add the shallots and orange zest and stir briefly to combine.

Preheat the oven to 375°F.

Spread half of the potato puree in the bottom of a 9-inch deep-dish pie pan and top with the grape mixture. Follow with the shredded duck, and then spread the remaining potato puree on top. Bake until the top is slightly browned and the pie is bubbling at the edges, 20 to 25 minutes.

Sprinkle the pie with the remaining teaspoon of thyme and a few cracks of pepper, if you like. Serve straightaway.

DUCK CONFIT

This tried-and-true old-fashioned recipe is one that I couldn't resist sharing again because one, it is the highlight of my Farmhouse Pie on page 146, and two, it's simply a fantastic preparation that borders on kitchen staple because of how versatile it is and how well it keeps. Is it fussier than making a roast chicken? In some ways, yes. But if you, like me, make a double batch to stash in the fridge, you'll be minutes away from roasting it with vegetables, baking it into a savory pie, panfrying it and serving it with a salad tossed in bright vinaigrette, shredding it over stews, or piling it on toast.

¼ cup herbes de Provence

¼ cup kosher salt

4 garlic cloves, sliced

1 large shallot, sliced

6 duck legs (about 5 pounds total)

4 cups rendered duck fat, melted, plus more as needed (see Cook's Note)

Neutral oil, such as canola or vegetable, for deep-frying

IN A LARGE BOWL, combine the herbs, salt, garlic, and shallot. Add the duck legs and rub the mixture all over them. Cover and let the duck cure in the refrigerator for 24 hours.

Preheat the oven to 250°F.

Gently brush the salt mixture from the duck legs and set them in a ceramic or glass baking dish big enough to accommodate them in a single layer. Pour in the duck fat so the legs are submerged, adding more if necessary. Bake until the duck is light golden and cooked through, about 4 hours.

Remove the duck from the oven and allow to cool to room temperature still submerged in the fat.

If you're serving the confit the same day you've prepared it, remove the duck from the fat, transfer it to a cooling rack set on a baking sheet, and refrigerate for an hour to dry out slightly. Discard the fat.

If serving the duck another day, leave the legs completely submerged in the fat and refrigerate. Because the duck is cured at this point and will be preserved in the duck fat, it will keep in the refrigerator for a few months. The beauty of confit—aka preserving the old-fashioned way!

When ready to serve the confit, heat a couple inches of oil in a deep fryer or large, deep skillet to 375°F. Remove the duck legs from the fat and, working in batches, fry until golden brown and warmed through, 3 to 4 minutes.

Drain the legs briefly on paper towels to absorb excess fat, then serve.

COOK'S NOTE: You can find duck fat in some grocery stores or order it online.

SKILLET CUTLETS
with Fennel Pollen & Mustard

Chicken breasts get a bad rap when it comes to choice pieces from the whole bird, but if they are dredged and panfried to a golden crisp and served with mustard, a heavy hand of Parmesan, and floral-yet-savory fennel pollen, there isn't a thigh or a leg you could trade me for them. If you are entertaining, you can prepare almost everything ahead of time, then just fry up the cutlets when you are ready to serve. Make it a meal with a nice, fresh salad.

2 boneless, skinless chicken breasts

1 cup panko breadcrumbs

½ cup crushed cornflakes

1 tablespoon cornstarch

½ cup whole milk

1 large egg

2 tablespoons Dijon mustard

½ cup all-purpose flour

¼ cup dry mustard

Kosher salt and freshly ground
black pepper

1 tablespoon fennel pollen

Vegetable or canola oil, for shallow-frying

Maldon salt, for finishing

Lemon wedges, for serving

Shaved Parmesan, for serving

LET THE CHICKEN BREASTS come to room temperature for about 1 hour.

Cut the chicken breasts in half horizontally. Place a piece of chicken between two sheets of parchment and use a rolling pin to pound the chicken into a cutlet about ¼ inch thick. Transfer the cutlet to a plate and repeat with the remaining chicken.

In a shallow bowl, combine the panko, cornflakes, and cornstarch. In another shallow bowl, whisk together the milk, egg, and Dijon. In a third bowl, mix the flour and dry mustard.

Season each cutlet on both sides with salt, a twist or two of pepper, and a generous ½ teaspoon of the fennel pollen, pressing the spices into the meat. Dredge one of the cutlets in the mustard and flour mixture, followed by the milk and egg mixture, followed by the cornflake-panko mixture, and place on a plate. Repeat with the remaining cutlets.

In a large, shallow skillet, heat ¼ inch of oil to 375°F over medium heat. Carefully lay the cutlets in the hot oil, working in batches if necessary, and cook, turning once, until golden brown on both sides, about 2 minutes per side. Transfer the fried cutlets to a baking sheet lined with paper towels. While the cutlets are still hot, sprinkle with Maldon salt and the remaining fennel pollen.

Serve with lemon wedges, topped with shaved Parmesan.

SAUCES
&
STAPLES

TO PREPARE, TO ELEVATE

Shallot Dressing 157

Floral Vinegar 158

Simple Buttermilk Dressing 159

Fresh Herb Oil 160

Kitchen Sink Pesto 162

Caper & Parsley Spoon Sauce 163

Garlicky Mayonnaise 164

Sour Cream from Scratch 165

Whipped Butters 166

Brown Butter 168

Basic Breadcrumbs 169

Roasted Chicken Stock 170

Learning how to cook at the diner instilled in me a deep appreciation for simplicity. Whether it's the technique I choose to execute a dish, the selection of ingredients I use, the number of dishes that will need to be dirtied, even the amount of movement required—it's all about keeping it simple. Simple is more efficient, yes, but it's also more centered. It allows me to cut directly to the heart of the matter, whether it's teasing out the flavor of an ingredient or connecting with the joy of the moment.

One of the keys to that simplicity is being prepared with an arsenal of basic kitchen staples that add instant flavor, dimension, and thoughtfulness to whatever it is you're cooking. Just one splash of shallot-infused vinegar (see page 157) can bring all the other elements of a dish into sharp, savory focus; homemade breadcrumbs (page 169) are a decadent, buttery condiment in their own right when scattered over pretty much anything; and a caper and parsley spoon sauce (page 163) requires no more effort than just roasting a chicken or some vegetables, because its burst of briny freshness is what's going to make the dish special and very, very delicious. These are the small touches that always give me confidence in the kitchen, because I know they're going to make whatever I'm preparing shine.

I call for these building blocks throughout the book in other recipes, but I highly recommend having a few of them made and at the ready. You'll be amazed at how effortlessly they'll become woven into your everyday repertoire.

SHALLOT DRESSING

This is my go-to magic vinaigrette. It is single-handedly responsible for making fresh ingredients taste like themselves, only better, and is basically the Swiss Army knife of condiments. Just a splash of it can add mouthwatering dimension to a potato salad, bring together a slaw, and make oysters taste even more like the ocean. I honestly don't know what I'd do without shallots and seasoned rice wine vinegar in my kitchen.

¼ cup finely chopped shallots

¼ cup seasoned rice wine vinegar

IN A SMALL BOWL, combine the shallots and vinegar. Let the mixture sit for at least 15 minutes for the shallots to soften and the flavors to meld. The sauce will keep covered in the refrigerator for a few days.

VINAIGRETTE VARIATIONS

I often use this mixture as the foundation for a salad dressing by whisking in 2 tablespoons extra-virgin olive oil and a few cracks of black pepper.

FOR A MUSTARD VINAIGRETTE, add a tablespoon of Dijon mustard.

FOR A HONEY VINAIGRETTE, add a tablespoon of honey.

FOR A CITRUSY VINAIGRETTE, add a couple of teaspoons of citrus zest and a squeeze of juice.

FOR A SPICED VINAIGRETTE, add a teaspoon of ground cumin or curry powder.

FOR AN HERBED VINAIGRETTE, add 2 teaspoons chopped soft fresh herbs, such as dill, tarragon, basil, or chives.

FOR MIGNONETTE SAUCE FOR OYSTERS

Add a few cracks of black pepper to the macerated shallots and refrigerate until nice and cold. **(MAKES ABOUT ⅓ CUP)**

MIGNONETTE VARIATIONS
(you can find even more of these on page 25)

1 tablespoon peeled and finely chopped apple plus 1 teaspoon finely chopped fresh chives

1 tablespoon finely chopped blueberries

1 tablespoon minced favorite soft fresh herb(s): tarragon, chives, dill, and/or basil

A few shakes of hot sauce

FLORAL VINEGAR

I was trying to come up with a sauce to complement a scallop dish when I realized that lilacs happened to be in season. On a lark, I stuffed a bunch of the petals into some seasoned rice wine vinegar and left them to marinate overnight. The combination of their distinct floral flavor and the sweet-tart vinegar was like nothing I'd ever tasted. People said those were the best scallops they ever had, but it was all the vinegar. Now I love making this simple and surprising condiment with all manner of flowers because of the way it somehow manages to both highlight the taste of what you're eating and add a little can't-quite-place-it note. Use infused vinegars for vinaigrettes, mignonettes, crudos, and pickles.

1 cup packed flower petals (see Cook's Note)

1 cup seasoned rice wine vinegar

IN A LARGE MASON JAR, combine the petals and vinegar, pushing the petals down until they are fully submerged. Cover and refrigerate for at least 2 days, and up to 1 week.

Strain out the petals, squeezing out any remaining liquid back into the vinegar, and return the vinegar to the jar. This will keep in the refrigerator for up to 1 month.

COOK'S NOTE: Some of my favorite flowers to infuse in vinegar are roses, hyssop, lilacs, purple violets, and white pennies.

SIMPLE BUTTERMILK DRESSING

This is your one-stop tangy, creamy dressing that doubles as a dip. Drizzle it over salads or serve it with crudités or fried chicken for dunking.

1½ cups Sour Cream from Scratch (page 165) or store-bought sour cream

2 tablespoons buttermilk

2 teaspoons fresh lemon juice

½ teaspoon kosher salt

Freshly ground black pepper

IN A MEDIUM BOWL, whisk together the sour cream, buttermilk, lemon juice, salt, and a few cracks of pepper. Refrigerate in an airtight container for up to 1 week.

MAKE IT YOUR OWN: For a bit of herbal flair, consider stirring in 2 tablespoons of chopped dill, basil, or chives. Tarragon is also lovely in this, but consider adding only 1 tablespoon because of its stronger flavor.

FRESH HERB OIL

Sprinkled over soups or sauces, or dotted onto dinner plates, this oil is a wonderful way to give your dishes a punch of bright color and flavor. Try dill or parsley oil with chowders or fish, or a ribbon of mint oil over a dish of lamb or lentil stew.

2 tablespoons plus ½ teaspoon kosher salt

2 cups packed soft fresh herb leaves, such as basil, tarragon, chives, parsley, mint, or dill

1 cup extra-virgin olive oil

PREPARE AN ICE BATH by filling a large bowl with a couple handfuls of ice and cold water.

In a large pot, combine 6 cups water and 2 tablespoons of the salt and bring to a boil over high heat. Carefully drop in the herbs and blanch for just 10 to 15 seconds, until they turn bright green. Quickly skim out the herbs and transfer them to the ice bath to stop the cooking. Then, using your hands, remove the herbs from the ice bath and squeeze out as much moisture as possible.

In a blender, combine the herbs, oil, and the remaining ½ teaspoon salt and blend until smooth. Let the oil sit for 30 minutes for the flavors to infuse.

Strain into a small bowl or spouted measuring cup, then pour the herb oil into a jar. The herb oil will keep in the sealed jar in the refrigerator for up to 1 week.

KITCHEN SINK PESTO

A dab of pesto adds instant depth of flavor and freshness to almost any dish, and the best part is that you can make pesto with more than just basil (although you could do just that with this recipe, and you would not be wrong). Many of the unsung heroes of the crisper bin—radish greens, broccoli greens, beet greens, carrot tops, and turnip greens—offer an equally delicious and verdant alternative. Made into pesto, they'll lend your roasted vegetables, fish, chicken, steak, cheeses, pasta, polenta, and eggs a savory boost, and, in exchange, you've saved them from the compost bin.

2 tablespoons pine nuts

2 cups packed fresh greens, such as radish, broccoli, or beet greens, carrot tops, or turnip greens

1 garlic clove, peeled

⅓ cup freshly grated Parmesan cheese

¼ cup extra-virgin olive oil

Juice of ½ lemon

½ teaspoon kosher salt

Freshly ground black pepper

IN A SMALL SKILLET, toast the pine nuts over low heat, stirring frequently, until fragrant and just beginning to brown, 2 to 3 minutes. Remove the pan from the heat and transfer the nuts to a plate to cool completely.

In the bowl of a food processor, combine the greens, cooled pine nuts, and garlic and pulse until well ground, like fine crumbs, but not turning into a paste. Add the Parmesan and pulse to mix. With the motor running, stream in the olive oil, followed by the lemon juice. Add the salt and a few cracks of pepper, taste, and adjust the seasoning if needed.

This will keep in an airtight container in the refrigerator for up to 3 days.

CAPER & PARSLEY SPOON SAUCE

Crispy, fresh parsley and briny, salty capers are more than the sum of their parts when blended into a pesto-like condiment. This sauce has the ability to transform the simplest of suppers into a luxurious offering that tastes like it took far longer to prepare. And, just as the name suggests, all you need to do is spoon it right over whatever you are serving. I especially love it dolloped and dribbled over chicken, fish, and vegetables.

½ cup packed fresh flat-leaf parsley leaves

2 tablespoons brine-packed capers

Grated zest and juice of 1 lemon

¼ cup extra-virgin olive oil

Freshly ground black pepper

USING A MORTAR AND pestle or a food processor, combine the parsley leaves, capers, and lemon zest and juice and process to a rough paste. Slowly drizzle in the olive oil, whisking to combine. Add a few cracks of pepper and blend well.

This can be stored in an airtight container in the refrigerator for up to 2 days.

GARLICKY MAYONNAISE

Since my fridge is usually overflowing with eggs from my chicken coop, I'm always looking for ways to make sure that they get put to good use. Making mayonnaise is one my favorite solutions—it's not only so much easier than you'd think thanks to a food processor, but it also has a lightness and brightness that store-bought mayo just doesn't provide. I always get a kick out of how downright elegant this spread can feel when it's prepared from scratch.

1 large egg plus 1 large egg yolk

1 large garlic clove, crushed and peeled

½ teaspoon kosher salt, or more to taste

2 cups vegetable or canola oil

Juice of 1 lemon

IN THE BOWL OF a food processor, combine the egg, yolk, garlic, and salt and process until the mixture is pale and creamy, about 1 minute. With the machine running, begin to add the oil one drop at a time, about one second at a time. It's important to start very slowly so the oil can emulsify; after a minute, you can start adding the oil a bit faster. Continue processing until the mixture has thickened, 4 to 5 minutes. Add the lemon juice and ¼ cup water and process until smooth. Taste for seasoning, and add more salt, if necessary.

I like using this the day it's made, but you can store a batch in an airtight container in the refrigerator for a day or two.

SOUR CREAM FROM SCRATCH

Maybe more than any other kitchen staple, there's something about home-made sour cream—or crème fraîche, if you're feeling fancy—that has the ability to improve just about anything you're serving. It's not so much that it's better than any product you can buy at the store—although that's absolutely true, both for its fresh, tangy taste and its luscious texture—but that it adds an extra-special touch. A simple baked potato served hot and crispy-skinned from the oven becomes a sumptuous meal with just a drizzle. Seasonal fruit baked in a rustic crust is transformed into an artisanal dessert. Homemade sour cream with fresh herbs is alchemized into the perfect dressing for raw or roasted vegetables. You get the idea. The only real challenge is not letting on just how easy this is to make.

3 cups heavy cream

⅓ cup buttermilk (well shaken before measuring)

IN A GLASS JAR, combine the cream and buttermilk. Cover the jar with a piece of cheesecloth or a paper towel, using a rubber band to secure it, and let sit at room temperature for 2 days, until thickened.

Cover the jar with an airtight lid and refrigerate for up to 3 weeks.

WHIPPED BUTTERS

There's no other way to put it: Butter Is Life. It is my desert-island ingredient, my security blanket in the kitchen, and the secret to so many delicious-tasting things. Plain butter from the happiest cows you can find is always going to be the ticket, and whipping good butter with all manner of inclusions, from herbs to spices to flower petals, is just about the easiest way to add something exceptional to an otherwise simple meal. Slather a knob of one of the savory combinations suggested below over chicken, steak, fish, or vegetables. Or try the sweeter version on grilled bread, biscuits, and scones. A batch lasts a couple weeks in the fridge, giving you the ability to pull together surprisingly complex-tasting dishes in minutes.

½ pound (2 sticks) unsalted butter, room temperature

½ teaspoon Maldon salt

IN THE BOWL OF a stand mixer fitted with the paddle attachment, beat the butter on high speed until pale in color and fluffy, scraping down the sides of the bowl frequently. Add the salt plus ¼ cup water and beat until incorporated. Add one of the following flavoring options.

FOR HERB BUTTER

¼ cup chopped mixed fresh herbs, such as chives, dill, tarragon, and/or thyme

FOR HONEY LAVENDER BUTTER

2 tablespoons honey

1 teaspoon dried culinary lavender (if using fresh lavender, double the amount)

Grated zest of 1 orange

FOR FLOWER PETAL BUTTER

Sprinkle in enough whole calendula leaves, pansies, or, for a spicier version, chopped nasturtium leaves to prettily dot the butter. Adding 1 to 2 teaspoons of grated citrus zest would be delicious here too.

FOR CURRY BUTTER

1 teaspoon extra-virgin olive oil

¼ cup minced onion

¼ cup minced carrot

Kosher salt

1 tablespoon curry powder

IN A SMALL SKILLET, heat the olive oil over medium heat. Add the onion and carrot and sprinkle with kosher salt to taste. Cook until the vegetables are tender, about 3 minutes, then add the curry and cook for 1 more minute, stirring constantly. Remove the pan from the heat and cool completely before beating the mixture into the whipped butter.

FOR CARAMELIZED ONION BUTTER

1 teaspoon extra-virgin olive oil

1 cup thinly sliced onion

Kosher salt

1 tablespoon unsalted butter

IN A SMALL SAUCEPAN, heat the olive oil over low heat. Add the onion and a sprinkle of salt and cook, stirring occasionally, until deep brown in color, 10 to 12 minutes. Add the butter and cook for 1 minute, until it melts. Remove the pan from the heat and let the onion cool completely before beating them into the whipped butter.

BROWN BUTTER

Simply put, brown butter is liquid gold. It's toasty, caramelized, decadent goodness that can be drizzled over potatoes, vegetables, or fish or folded into cake batters. You can pretty much use this wherever regular butter applies, which is . . . everywhere.

4 tablespoons unsalted butter

IN A SMALL SAUCEPAN, cook the butter over medium-low heat, stirring occasionally, until it starts to foam and brown bits start to form on the bottom of the pan, 3 to 4 minutes. The milk solids can burn quickly, so keep a close eye as you stir! Immediately remove the butter from the heat and pour it into a heatproof bowl to stop the cooking.

Use immediately in liquid form, or transfer the butter to an airtight container and store in a cool place for up to 3 days.

BASIC BREADCRUMBS

You have most likely heard it before: breadcrumbs you make at home are always going to have better texture and flavor than store-bought. But I'd go a step further and say that the dry, sawdusty imposters in the canister you can buy off the shelf shouldn't even be considered in the same category. Bits of good bread not quite fresh enough for sandwiches or toast that you've ground up and sautéed in butter until crispy are in a class all their own, as much a condiment as they are a crunchy sprinkle. I love adding these over a little salad with a wedge of cheese, or scattering them over fish, or side dishes—or anything.

4 cups cubed day-old crusty bread

1 tablespoon unsalted butter

Maldon salt

PREHEAT THE OVEN TO 250°F.

Spread the bread cubes in a single layer on a baking sheet and bake until completely dried out, about 1 hour.

Transfer the bread to the bowl of a food processor and pulse until coarsely ground. Store the breadcrumbs in an airtight container in your pantry for up to 1 month.

When you're ready to use the breadcrumbs, melt the butter in a small skillet over medium heat. Add the breadcrumbs, toss to coat, and toast until golden, 3 to 4 minutes. Add a pinch of Maldon salt and toss to combine. Done!

ROASTED CHICKEN STOCK

MAKES 3 QUARTS

I know what you're thinking: *Yeah, yeah, I'll just buy it at the store.* But hear me out: something almost otherworldly happens to a stock that's made with roasted chicken, bones and all. It gets rich and deeply flavorful, which in turn makes anything you're cooking that much more delicious (another shout-out to bone marrow!). Trust me, I'd be the first to tell you to keep it simple. But when you're working with few ingredients and doing as little to them as possible, every layer of flavor counts. From providing a flawless starting point for soups, stews, and risottos to deglazing the browned bits in the bottom of a pan to make a sauce, this stock delivers something store-bought stock just can't compete with.

1 whole chicken

2 large onions, peeled and quartered

2 tablespoons kosher salt

1 teaspoon freshly ground black pepper

4 dried bay leaves

PREHEAT THE OVEN TO 450°F.

Start by cutting the chicken into pieces so it's easier to work with: Remove the breasts and reserve for a later use (see Cook's Note). Using a cleaver or a very large knife, break down the remaining pieces, making sure to crack all the bones to help release the marrow.

Spread the chicken pieces and onion quarters evenly on a baking sheet and season with the salt and pepper. Roast for 15 minutes.

Carefully transfer the roasted chicken pieces and onions, plus any roasty bits from the pan, to a large stockpot. Add the bay leaves and 12 quarts of water and bring the water to a boil over high heat. Reduce the heat to medium and simmer for 4 to 5 hours, until the liquid is reduced by at least half.

Strain the stock through a fine-mesh strainer into a large container or bowl and discard the chicken, onions, and bay leaves. Allow the stock to cool completely, then cover and refrigerate overnight.

The next day, skim off any fat that has formed on the top of the stock. Transfer to several airtight containers and freeze for up to 6 months, or store in the refrigerator for up to 1 week.

COOK'S NOTE: This stock is all about dark meat and bones, so I call for removing the breasts and reserving them for another use—such as enjoying them for dinner the night you prep this stock (perhaps in Skillet Cutlets with Fennel Pollen and Mustard, page 151).

SWEETS

TO CELEBRATE, TO INDULGE, TO DELIGHT

Cream Puffs with Salted Caramel Sauce 177

Glazed Butter Cake 179

Cloud Whip with Fresh Berries 183

Lemon Gingersnap Icebox Pie 184

Rose Panna Cotta 187

Roasted Peach Pie with Almond & Fennel 188

Old-Fashioned Apple Walnut Cake 192

Salted Caramel Custards 195

Vanilla Bean Custard Sauce 196

Sweet Cream Ice Cream 197

Brown-Buttered Pecan Cookies 198

Chocolate Ginger'd Cookies 201

Chocolate Coins with Candied Ginger,
Almonds & Rose 202

Dried Cherry, Cornmeal & Almond Cookies 204

Dessert is a universal language. We make sweet treats to mark special occasions, to show that we care, to bring comfort, and to scratch an itch. They are also a thread that we all have running through our lives, back to when we were kids. The fresh doughnuts after a soccer game, the largest slab of cake you could finagle on your birthday, the soft-serve ice cream on a summer evening, the pie that grandma always used to make—these indelible memories connect us with a tender part of ourselves. They are, no matter what else may have been going on at that time or since, sweet. To serve someone dessert is to touch those memories—something I don't take lightly. Whether it's a rose-scented panna cotta (page 187), a delicately glazed buttery cake (page 179), or a bowl of berries draped in freshly whipped cream (page 183), my goal is always to make guests feel cared for and just a little bit spoiled—as if they could want for nothing more.

CREAM PUFFS
with Salted Caramel Sauce

This recipe is a shout-out to my mom's regular Wednesday-night special: cream puffs with ice cream and chocolate syrup. It was the ultimate proof that even with a handful of no-frills ingredients—flour, butter, sugar—you can create something really exceptional. Our version involved Breyer's ice cream and Hershey's chocolate syrup, and I'm certainly not too good for these old-school classics, but you could take things to the next level by making your own Sweet Cream Ice Cream (page 197) and salted caramel sauce. Whichever way you go, this is still one of the least fancy fancy desserts there are.

FOR THE SALTED CARAMEL SAUCE

1 cup granulated sugar

3½ tablespoons unsalted butter

¾ cup heavy cream

1 teaspoon kosher salt

FOR THE CREAM PUFFS

1 cup whole milk

8 tablespoons (1 stick) unsalted butter

1 tablespoon granulated sugar

1 teaspoon kosher salt

1 cup all-purpose flour

4 large eggs

1 teaspoon vanilla extract

Sweet Cream Ice Cream (page 197) or your favorite store-bought ice cream, for serving (optional)

MAKE THE CARAMEL SAUCE: In a medium heavy-bottomed saucepan, combine the sugar with ¼ cup water, bring to a boil over medium-high heat, and boil undisturbed until the mixture turns golden brown, about 5 minutes. Don't stir during this time, just shake the pan occasionally to encourage even coloring. Add the butter and whisk to combine. Add the cream—it will bubble and steam aggressively; be careful not to burn yourself—and whisk until smooth and incorporated, about 1 minute. Whisk in the salt and remove the pan from the heat.

Cover the pan and keep the sauce warm until ready to serve, or allow the sauce to cool and transfer it to an airtight container. It will keep in the refrigerator for up to 1 week.

-recipe continues-

COOK'S NOTE: To freeze any extra puffs, place them on a parchment paper–lined baking sheet and freeze until completely frozen, about 2 hours. Transfer the puffs to a freezer bag to store for up to 3 months. When ready to use, defrost the puffs in the refrigerator overnight or at room temperature for about 2 hours. Split and toast the puffs in a toaster or heat in a 375°F oven for 2 to 4 minutes.

MAKE THE CREAM PUFFS: Preheat the oven to 375°F. Line a baking sheet with parchment paper or a Silpat and set aside.

In a medium saucepan, combine the milk, butter, sugar, and salt and bring to a simmer over medium-high heat; use a wooden spoon to stir as the butter melts, about 2 minutes. Add the flour and stir quickly to combine, then continue stirring until the mixture pulls away from the sides of the pan and forms a ball, about 30 seconds.

Transfer the dough to the bowl of a food processor. With the motor running, add the eggs one at a time, processing until each one is incorporated, then add the vanilla, processing just until all the ingredients are fully incorporated and the batter is smooth. Remove from the food processor bowl and transfer the dough to a piping bag fitted with a ½-inch plain tip.

Pipe the dough into 2-inch dollops onto the prepared baking sheet, leaving about 2 inches between them. Bake until puffed and golden brown, rotating the pan halfway through, 20 to 24 minutes.

For a Wednesday-night special, serve the warm cream puffs with ice cream, if desired, and the caramel sauce and let people assemble their own. (If serving ice cream, be sure to provide a knife for them to slice into their puffs in order to tuck the ice cream inside.) For a more polished occasion, offer a platter of composed cream puffs: either split the cream puffs open, add a small scoop of ice cream to each, and serve with the sauce; or skip the ice cream and drizzle the platterful of cream puffs with the sauce.

GLAZED BUTTER CAKE

Ask me what my favorite ingredient is, and I'll tell you again and again: butter. Maybe it was the stick of butter on the table at every family meal, ready to be slathered on slices of white bread, dolloped onto mashed potatoes, or melted over a hot stack of pancakes. Maybe it was the stick upon stick called for in the cookies and cakes I'd bake with my gram. Or maybe it's just good sense. Butter has had a special place in my heart for as long as I can remember. So when it came to making an uncomplicated, timeless dessert that felt so very, well, me—it had to be all about butter. This is really the only cake you need in your repertoire. Serve it sliced thick with strawberries and cream, or topped with lemon curd and blueberries, or perfectly plain with a hot cup of tea alongside.

FOR THE CAKE

8 tablespoons (1 stick) unsalted butter, at room temperature, plus more for the pan

1½ cups all-purpose flour, plus more for the pan

1 cup granulated sugar

2 large eggs

½ teaspoon baking powder

½ teaspoon baking soda

½ teaspoon kosher salt

½ cup buttermilk (well shaken before measuring)

1 teaspoon vanilla extract

FOR THE GLAZE

1 cup granulated sugar

8 tablespoons (1 stick) unsalted butter

2 teaspoons vanilla extract

1 teaspoon almond extract

MAKE THE CAKE: Preheat the oven to 350°F. Butter and flour a 9-inch loaf pan, line with parchment paper, and set aside.

In the bowl of a stand mixer fitted with the paddle attachment, beat the butter and sugar on high speed until light and fluffy, about 5 minutes. Add the eggs one at a time, incorporating the first egg before adding the second one.

In a medium bowl, whisk together the flour, baking powder, baking soda, and salt.

With the mixer on low, one large spoonful at a time, alternate adding the dry mixture and the buttermilk, mixing until well combined. Add the vanilla and mix just briefly to combine.

Pour the batter into the prepared loaf pan and bake until the cake is golden and a cake tester inserted in the center comes out clean, 20 to 25 minutes.

-recipe continues-

MAKE THE GLAZE: In a small saucepan, combine the sugar, butter, and ¼ cup water and bring the mixture to a boil over medium-high heat, whisking occasionally. Remove the pan from the heat and let the glaze cool slightly, then whisk in the vanilla and almond extracts. The glaze will cool and thicken a bit as it sits.

For a quick and rustic finish, brush the glaze over the top of the loaf in the pan. Allow the cake to cool completely, remove from the pan, and slice. Or, to really allow the cake to soak up all the delicious glaze, let the cake cool in the pan until it's comfortable to handle. Remove the cake and transfer to a cooling rack set over a baking sheet, to catch the drips of glaze. Brush the glaze over the entire cake: top, bottom, and, sides. You will need to work gently and carefully, but it's worth it to get every inch of this cake covered in glaze. Repeat until all of the glaze has been used.

Let the cake cool completely, then wrap tightly and store on the counter for up to 3 days.

CLOUD WHIP with Fresh Berries

Most of my recipes are pulled directly from what I loved as a kid: fry baskets, lobster boils, meat loaf, mashed potatoes, soft-serve, pretty much anything in a cast-iron skillet, cinnamon buns from a can, and, in this case, Cool-Whip. I used to love eating spoonfuls straight from the container—just one of the many ways that my grandmother would spoil me. I've given this classic treat a makeover using whole ingredients, but it's still pure, cloud-like goodness ideal for dolloping alongside the summer's best berries.

5 large eggs, separated

1 cup granulated sugar

1 vanilla bean, split lengthwise, seeds scraped out and reserved (pod discarded or saved for another use)

Pinch of kosher salt

2 cups heavy cream

Fresh berries, such as raspberries, strawberries, or blueberries, for serving

FILL A LARGE BOWL with a couple handfuls of ice and cold water and set aside.

Place the egg yolks in a medium heat-proof bowl and add ½ cup of the sugar, the vanilla seeds, and 2 tablespoons water.

In a medium saucepan, bring a few inches of water to a simmer over medium-high heat. Set the bowl with the yolks over the saucepan, making sure it is not touching the water. Using a hand mixer, whip the yolks on low speed until the mixture becomes frothy, about 4 minutes. Transfer the bowl to the prepared ice bath and beat the mixture on high speed until pale and thick, about 8 minutes. Remove the bowl from the ice bath and set aside.

In the bowl of a stand mixer fitted with the whisk attachment, whip the egg whites on high speed until stiff peaks form, about 4 minutes. Slowly add the remaining ½ cup sugar and then the salt and continue to whip until incorporated, another minute or so. Transfer the whipped egg whites to the bowl with the yolk mixture and gently fold in with a silicone spatula to combine.

Add the heavy cream to the mixer bowl—no need to wash it out first—and whip the cream on high speed just until stiff, about 4 minutes. Fold the whipped cream into the egg mixture.

To serve, spoon the cloud cream into bowls and top with fresh berries.

COOK'S NOTE: If you don't have a vanilla bean on hand, you can substitute vanilla extract. Just add a teaspoon of it to the whipped cream. The cloud cream is best enjoyed fresh but can be refrigerated and served later in the day.

MAKE IT YOUR OWN: For a citrusy mousse, substitute fresh lemon juice or orange juice for the water. This dessert is also delicious frozen: Line a loaf pan with plastic wrap, fill it with the cloud cream, and freeze overnight, then unmold and slice. Top with berries and serve.

LEMON GINGERSNAP ICEBOX PIE

What I love about this pie—aside from the fact that it's no-bake except for the crust—is how well suited it is for both warm- and cold-weather occasions. It's cool and creamy, yet the citrus-ginger combination is also fitting for the fall or winter. I suggest making this pie the day before you plan to serve it, then slicing it straight from the freezer.

FOR THE CRUST

1 box gingersnap cookies (about 9 ounces)

¼ cup granulated sugar

4 tablespoons unsalted butter, melted

FOR THE FILLING

6 large egg yolks

¼ cup granulated sugar

Pinch of kosher salt

1 (14-ounce) can sweetened condensed milk

2 tablespoons grated lemon zest

¾ cup fresh lemon juice

Freshly whipped cream, for serving

MAKE THE CRUST: Preheat the oven to 350°F.

In the bowl of a food processor, pulse the cookies until the crumbs are the consistency of coarse sand. Transfer the crumbs to a medium bowl, add the sugar and melted butter, and stir to combine.

Pour the crust mixture into a 9-inch springform pan or pie dish and press evenly over the bottom of the pan. Bake until just barely golden and puffed, 8 to 10 minutes. Set aside to cool completely before adding the filling.

MAKE THE FILLING: In the bowl of a stand mixer fitted with the whisk attachment, combine the egg yolks, sugar, and salt and whip on high speed until the mixture is light in color, 3 to 4 minutes. With the mixer running, slowly add the sweetened condensed milk, and then the lemon zest and juice.

Pour the filling into the prepared pan and freeze for at least 6 hours, or up to overnight.

If using a springform pan, unmold the pie. Slice into wedges and serve with freshly whipped cream.

ROSE PANNA COTTA

SERVES 6

It always surprises people to know that my ideal sweet treat doesn't involve chocolate. Give me something rich, creamy, and custardy over anything chocolate, any day. Panna cotta, the eggless cousin of custard, falls into that category, and the recipe is so simple that I hope it finds its way into your regular repertoire. This version, which is infused with a soft rose essence, may sound dressed-up, but I assure you that it's more than comfortable being served casually, especially with fresh berries and a drizzle of honey.

FOR THE PANNA COTTA

2 sheets gelatin

2 cups heavy cream

¼ cup granulated sugar

1 vanilla bean, split lengthwise, seeds scraped out, seeds and pod reserved

Pinch of kosher salt

¼ cup rosewater

FOR SERVING

Fresh strawberries or raspberries

Honey

Edible flowers (I love pansies or rose petals for this one, optional)

MAKE THE PANNA COTTA: Put the gelatin in a shallow bowl, cover with ice water, and set aside to soak for 15 minutes to soften.

Fill a large bowl halfway with ice. Nest a medium bowl into the ice and top it with a sieve. Set aside.

In a medium saucepan, combine the cream, sugar, vanilla seeds and pod, and salt and, whisking frequently, bring the mixture to a simmer over medium heat, being careful not to let it boil. Remove from the heat.

Squeeze out any excess liquid from the gelatin sheets, add them to the cream mixture, and whisk until the sheets have dissolved.

Pour the hot cream mixture through the sieve into the bowl in the ice bath. Discard the vanilla bean. Let the mixture cool in the ice bath, whisking occasionally, for 5 to 10 minutes. Stir the rosewater into the cooled cream mixture.

Divide the cream among six 6-ounce ramekins. Cover and refrigerate for at least 6 hours, or up to overnight.

TO SERVE: Have fun with it! Garnish each panna cotta with fresh berries, a drizzle of honey, and edible flowers.

ROASTED PEACH PIE
with Almond & Fennel

I'll see your traditional peach pie and raise you an open-faced, sugar-crusted crostata that allows the peaches to get even more deeply caramelized and scented with sweet, herbaceous fennel. It's a breezy summer pie at heart, and it's still going to light up those memories of backyard barbecues and the juices of farmers' market peaches dribbling down your chin.

FOR THE CRUST

1½ cups all-purpose flour,
plus more for dusting

1 tablespoon granulated sugar

½ teaspoon kosher salt

1½ sticks cold unsalted butter,
cut into tablespoon-sized pieces

⅓ cup ice water

FOR THE FILLING

⅓ cup whole unblanched almonds,
toasted until fragrant and finely ground

¼ cup granulated sugar

3 tablespoons all-purpose flour

2 teaspoons ground fennel

6 peaches, halved, pitted, and
cut into ⅛-inch slices

1 tablespoon almond extract

2 tablespoons unsalted butter

½ teaspoon fennel pollen

Freshly whipped cream or Sweet Cream
Ice Cream (page 197), for serving
(optional)

MAKE THE CRUST: In the bowl of a food processor, combine the flour, sugar, and salt and pulse to blend. Add the butter and ice water and pulse until the mixture resembles cottage cheese.

Turn the dough out onto a lightly floured surface and use your hands to shape it into a ball. Try not to overwork the dough, or it will become tough.

Using a lightly floured rolling pin, roll the dough into a 14-inch round. Transfer it to a parchment paper–lined baking sheet, cover with plastic wrap, and chill in the refrigerator for at least 30 minutes, or up to overnight.

MAKE THE FILLING: Preheat the oven to 400°F.

In a medium bowl, combine the ground almonds, 3 tablespoons of the sugar, the flour, and the ground fennel. Spread the mixture over the center of the chilled dough, leaving a 2-inch border around the edges.

In another medium bowl, toss the peach slices with the almond extract. Starting from the outer edges of the nut mixture, lay the peach slices in concentric circles over it, working your way toward the middle. Fold the edges of the dough over the outer edges of the peaches. Dot the fruit with the butter and sprinkle the entire pie with the remaining tablespoon of sugar.

Bake until the fruit is bubbly and the crust is golden brown, about 20 minutes. Sprinkle the pie with the fennel pollen and let cool slightly before cutting.

Serve the pie with freshly whipped cream or scoops of ice cream, if you like.

OLD-FASHIONED APPLE WALNUT CAKE

Warm baking spices like cinnamon, nutmeg, and allspice bring me back to my mother's kitchen in November, when I would always help her make apple pie. It never failed to amaze me how the apples we'd bring home from the orchard were transformed into deeply sweet goo. Since that is my favorite part of the dessert, I've done away with the crust and brought the skillet-roasted apples front and center in this moist, walnut-studded cake.

3 cups ½-inch apple pieces
(such as Fuji or Lady Crisp)

2 tablespoons unsalted butter

1 tablespoon apple pie spice

¾ cup plus 1 tablespoon granulated sugar

2 cups all-purpose flour,
plus more for dusting

2 teaspoons ground cinnamon

2 teaspoons baking soda

1 teaspoon kosher salt

4 large eggs

¾ cup vegetable oil

⅔ cup packed brown sugar

Grated zest of 1 orange

1 cup walnut pieces

Powdered sugar, for sprinkling

Vanilla Bean Custard Sauce (page 196) or freshly whipped cream, for serving

PREHEAT THE OVEN TO 350°F. Grease a 10-inch Bundt pan with butter and lightly dust with flour, turning the pan upside down and gently tapping to remove any excess flour.

In a medium skillet, combine the apples, butter, pie spice, and 1 tablespoon of the sugar and cook over low heat, stirring frequently, until the apples are tender and just cooked through, about 5 minutes. Remove the pan from the heat.

In a medium bowl, whisk together the flour, cinnamon, baking soda, and salt; set aside.

In the bowl of a stand mixer fitted with the paddle attachment, combine the eggs, vegetable oil, the remaining ¾ cup granulated sugar, the brown sugar, and orange zest and beat on medium speed until thoroughly blended, about 1 minute. With the mixer on low speed, slowly add the flour mixture. Fold in the warm apples and the walnuts and pour the batter into the prepared pan.

Bake for 45 to 50 minutes, until a cake tester inserted in the middle of the cake comes out clean. Invert the cake onto a cake plate, but leave the pan on the cake for 10 minutes.

Remove the pan and sprinkle the cake generously with powdered sugar. Slice and serve at room temperature with the custard sauce or whipped cream.

Wrapped tightly, this cake will stay moist in your bread box for 3 to 4 days.

SALTED CARAMEL CUSTARDS

SERVES 8

This is a love letter to all of the puddings that my mother and grandmother used to make. Maybe it's the nostalgia for the days when just about anything could be solved with something sweet, or maybe it's the wonder I'll always have for the way eggs, sugar, and cream can be transformed into a luscious, velvety, deeply caramel-flavored dessert, but either way, this recipe tugs at my heartstrings.

4 cups heavy cream

1 vanilla bean, split lengthwise, seeds scraped out, seeds and pod reserved

¾ cup granulated sugar

6 large egg yolks

½ teaspoon kosher salt

Boiling water, for the water bath

Freshly whipped cream, for serving

IN A MEDIUM SAUCEPAN, bring the cream to a slow simmer over low heat. Remove the pan from the heat, add the vanilla seeds and pod, and set aside to steep for 10 to 15 minutes. Remove the vanilla pod and discard or rinse and save for another use.

In a medium, heavy-bottomed pot, combine the sugar and ¼ cup water. Bring to a boil over high heat and boil until the mixture turns amber in color, about 5 minutes. Working quickly, whisk the cream mixture into the caramel, being careful, as it will bubble and steam, Then continue whisking the mixture over medium heat until smooth. Remove the pot from the heat and set aside to cool slightly.

In a medium bowl, whisk the egg yolks and salt until combined. Slowly whisk in the cream mixture until smooth, allow the mixture to cool slightly, then pour into an airtight container.

Refrigerate the custard mixture for at least 4 hours, or, ideally, overnight. Letting the custard sit overnight leads to a thicker, creamier custard.

Preheat the oven to 300°F. Set eight 6-ounce ramekins in a deep roasting pan.

Divide the custard mixture among the ramekins. Carefully add enough boiling water to the roasting pan to reach halfway up the sides of the ramekins. Cover with foil and bake until the custards are completely set, 40 to 50 minutes. Remove the pan from the oven and set the custards aside in the water bath.

When the custards are cool enough to handle, remove them from the water bath and let them cool completely. Transfer the custards to the refrigerator to chill for at least 3 hours.

Serve the custards topped with a dollop of freshly whipped cream. Or, if you are feeling adventurous, you can cover the tops with a thin layer of sugar and torch or broil for a dreamy crème brûlée.

VANILLA BEAN CUSTARD SAUCE

I'm a big believer in having a small trove of impossibly simple, tried-and-true recipes that can be mixed, matched, and riffed on depending on season and mood. Well, this is hands-down one of those recipes. My crisps, crumbles, and tarts are all very familiar with this sauce, as it's endlessly versatile and just a drizzle has the ability to make almost any dessert, including fresh fruit, more interesting and delicious. One of my favorite ways to serve it is in a small pitcher on the table so guests can help themselves, and generously so.

2 cups heavy cream

¼ cup granulated sugar

1 vanilla bean, split lengthwise, seeds scraped out, seeds and pod reserved

3 large egg yolks

Pinch of kosher salt

SET A FINE-MESH SIEVE over a medium bowl and set aside.

In a medium, heavy-bottomed saucepan, combine the cream, sugar, vanilla seeds, and vanilla pod and bring to a slow simmer over medium-high heat. Remove the pan from the heat and let the cream steep for at least 20 minutes. Remove the vanilla pod.

In a medium bowl, whisk the egg yolks and salt until combined. Very slowly add the warm cream mixture, whisking constantly. Add the custard mixture back to the saucepan, set the pan over medium heat, and whisk constantly until the custard begins to thicken—an instant-read thermometer should read between 160 and 165°F. Do not let the custard boil, or the eggs will cook and curdle. Remove the pan from the heat and immediately strain the custard through the sieve and let cool completely.

Store the custard sauce in an airtight container in the refrigerator for up to 1 week.

COOK'S NOTE: Fold a bit of the custard sauce into some stiffly whipped cream for a fluffy dessert. Scatter with fresh berries and enjoy.

MAKE IT YOUR OWN: Think of this basic custard sauce as a chance for your imagination to run wild. By steeping the cream with any number of teas, herbs, or flowers, you can completely transform it. Some ideas:

- Earl Grey tea
- Orange zest
- Fresh or dried lavender
- Fresh rosemary sprigs
- Chamomile
- Roses

SWEET CREAM ICE CREAM

When I was growing up, the official taste of summer was the vanilla soft-serve from the dairy bar window of the diner. No matter how exhausted I'd be from a day working on the line or how revved up my dad was about my making the cones too big for the customers—"two twists around for a tot, three for a small, five for a large!"—nothing compared to that cool, creamy cone. This recipe is sort of the grown-up version of it. It's elegant in its simplicity, showing off the flavor of a few high-quality ingredients.

1 sheet gelatin

1¾ cups whole milk

1¾ cups heavy cream

½ cup granulated sugar

⅓ cup nonfat milk powder

PUT THE GELATIN IN a shallow bowl, cover with ice water, and set aside to soak for 20 minutes to soften.

Meanwhile, in a small saucepan, whisk together the milk, cream, sugar, and milk powder. Set the pan over medium heat and bring to a slow simmer, whisking until the sugar dissolves, 2 to 3 minutes; be careful not to let the mixture boil. Remove the pan from the heat.

Remove the gelatin from the ice water, squeeze out the excess water, add the gelatin to the warm cream mixture, and whisk to dissolve. In a large bowl, combine a couple handfuls of ice with cold water. Set another large bowl over the top of the ice bath and strain the cream mixture through a fine-mesh sieve into the bowl. Allow the cream to cool completely, stirring occasionally. Remove the bowl from the ice bath, cover, and refrigerate overnight.

Churn the mixture in an ice cream maker according to the manufacturer's instructions until smooth and creamy.

Pack the ice cream into a freezer container, cover, and freeze for at least 4 hours before serving.

COOK'S NOTE: You'll notice that this recipe uses gelatin instead of eggs, which will give you the same creaminess but with fool-proof stability.

MAKE IT YOUR OWN: You can use this ice cream base as the canvas for all manner of flavorings and mix-ins. Steeping the milk with spices or herbs will unlock fun new flavors. Or swirl a few spoonfuls of jam into the freshly churned ice cream for a ripple effect. Here are a few steeping suggestions:

- Toasted fennel seeds
- Toasted coriander seeds
- Fresh rosemary sprigs
- Fresh or dried lavender
- Sliced fresh ginger
- Pink peppercorns
- Fresh basil leaves

BROWN-BUTTERED PECAN COOKIES

MAKES ABOUT 2 DOZEN SMALL COOKIES

I make these cookies smaller than I normally would because there's so much rich, decadent flavor packed into each bite, thanks to toasty brown butter, crunchy flecks of toffee, and a sprinkling of sea salt. Be sure to serve these with glasses of cold milk for dunking.

8 tablespoons (1 stick) unsalted butter

1¼ cup plus 2 tablespoons all-purpose flour

½ teaspoon baking powder

½ teaspoon kosher salt

½ teaspoon baking soda

½ cup packed brown sugar

¼ cup plus 1 tablespoon granulated sugar, plus more for rolling

1 large egg

1 teaspoon vanilla extract

¾ cup chopped milk chocolate toffee pieces

½ cup chopped pecans

Maldon salt, for sprinkling

IN A SMALL SAUCEPAN, cook the butter over medium-low heat, stirring occasionally, until the butter melts and starts to foam and brown bits begin to form on the bottom of the pan, about 8 minutes. The butter can burn quickly, so keep a close eye on it. Immediately remove the pan from the heat and pour the butter into a heatproof bowl. Cover and let the butter solidify in a cool spot, about 2 hours.

Preheat the oven to 350°F. Line two baking sheets with parchment paper and set aside.

In a medium bowl, whisk together the flour, baking powder, and salt; set aside.

In a small bowl, dissolve the baking soda into ½ tablespoon water and set aside.

In the bowl of a stand mixer fitted with the paddle attachment, combine the brown sugar, granulated sugar, and solidified brown butter and beat on high speed until light and fluffy, 4 to 5 minutes, scraping down the bowl as needed. Add the egg, beating until incorporated, then beat in the vanilla extract and the dissolved baking soda. Reduce the mixer speed to low and slowly add the flour mixture, beating until it's fully incorporated. Remove the bowl from the mixer stand, add the toffee bits, and fold them in until just combined.

Spread an even layer of sugar on a small plate. Using a 2-teaspoon cookie scoop or a spoon, form the dough into 1-inch balls, roll in the sugar to coat, and set on the prepared baking sheets, spacing them about 1½ inches apart. Using your fingers, gently press down on each dough ball to form it into a little puck. (This will help the cookies bake more evenly.) Sprinkle the flattened cookies with the chopped pecans and bake until golden, about 8 minutes. Remove from the oven.

While the cookies are still hot, sprinkle with Maldon salt. Let cool on the baking sheet for about 5 minutes.

These are best served warm, but the cooled cookies will keep in an airtight container for 3 to 5 days.

CHOCOLATE GINGER'D COOKIES

Chocolate and ginger are a sophisticated combination that brings a graceful close to a meal, but served warm (ideally with milk), these cookies also have a way of stirring your inner child.

1½ cups all-purpose flour

¼ cup Dutch-processed cocoa powder

1 teaspoon baking soda

½ teaspoon ground ginger

½ teaspoon ground cinnamon

¼ teaspoon kosher salt

Good pinch of ground cloves

1 cup granulated sugar, plus more for coating

8 tablespoons (1 stick) unsalted butter, at room temperature

1 large egg

¼ cup plus 2 tablespoons semisweet chocolate chips

¼ cup chopped candied ginger

Maldon salt, for sprinkling

IN A MEDIUM BOWL, whisk together the flour, cocoa, baking soda, ginger, cinnamon, salt, and cloves. Set aside.

In the bowl of a stand mixer fitted with the paddle attachment, beat the sugar and butter on high speed until light and fluffy, 4 to 5 minutes. Add the egg and beat until fully incorporated. Add the flour mixture and beat just until the dough comes together, another minute or so. Remove the bowl from the mixer stand and fold in the chocolate chips and candied ginger. Cover the dough with plastic wrap and refrigerate for 30 minutes.

Preheat the oven to 375°F. Line two baking sheets with parchment paper and set aside.

Fill a small bowl half-full with sugar. Using a 2-teaspoon cookie scoop or a spoon, form the dough into 1-inch balls. Roll the balls in the sugar to coat and arrange them on the prepared baking sheets, spacing them about 2 inches apart. Gently push down on each ball to flatten the cookies to about ½ inch thick. Bake until the cookies just begin to crack on top, 8 to 10 minutes. Remove from the oven.

Sprinkle the cookies with Maldon salt while they're still hot. Let them rest on the baking sheets for a few minutes.

These are best served warm, but the cooled cookies will keep in an airtight container for 3 to 5 days.

CHOCOLATE COINS
with Candied Ginger, Almonds & Rose

MAKES ABOUT 16 COINS

While chocolate may not be my dessert love language, I know that many people love ending their meals with it. These bites are just the thing for scratching the itch, but in a much more interesting way thanks to rose petals, candied ginger, and toasted almonds.

4 ounces bittersweet chocolate, chopped

1 tablespoon roughly chopped toasted almonds

1 tablespoon thin 1-inch-long strips candied ginger

1 tablespoon dried rose petals

Maldon salt, for sprinkling

LINE A BAKING SHEET with a Silpat or parchment paper and set aside.

In a medium saucepan, bring a few inches of water to a simmer over medium-high heat. Add the chocolate to a medium heatproof bowl and set the bowl over the saucepan so it nests a bit into the pan without touching the water. Melt the chocolate, stirring occasionally, until smooth. Remove the bowl from the heat.

Drop teaspoonfuls of the melted chocolate onto the lined baking sheet 2 inches apart. Shake the pan gently back and forth so the spoonfuls of chocolate flatten into coins. Arrange the almonds, ginger, and rose petals decoratively on top and sprinkle with Maldon salt. Refrigerate the coins for 10 minutes to set.

Store the chocolate coins in an airtight container at room temperature for up to 2 weeks.

MAKE IT YOUR OWN: These coins are perfect for changing up the flavor and texture. Dried fruits such as apricots and cherries would also be delicious, as would toasted hazelnuts, pecans, or peanuts.

A FEW MORE IDEAS:

• Serve scoops of Sweet Cream Ice Cream (page 197), or any ice cream you like, in tiny cones. I love my Nordic Ware Krumkake Iron for making mini waffle cones. You can make the cones ahead and store them in an airtight container.

• Freeze the lemonade base for the Thai Basil Lemonade (page 52) in ice-pop molds. Use traditional ice-pop sticks or the maple twigs from page 266.

• For a boozy float, put a scoop of Sorbet (page 55) in the bottom of each glass (such as a coupe or vintage cordial glass), top off with a splash of Prosecco, and add fresh herbs or edible flowers for garnish.

DRIED CHERRY, CORNMEAL & ALMOND COOKIES

It's the bite of the stone-ground cornmeal, crunch of the almonds, and tartness of the dried cherries that make this cookie a perfectly balanced after-dinner bite. Even the fullest of bellies has room for at least one. As always, the cookies are best served warm.

¾ cup granulated sugar, plus more for rolling

6 tablespoons unsalted butter, at room temperature

1 large egg

Grated zest of 1½ lemons

½ teaspoon vanilla extract

¼ teaspoon almond extract

1 cup all-purpose flour

5 tablespoons stone-ground cornmeal

½ teaspoon baking soda

½ teaspoon kosher salt

½ cup chopped dried cherries

¼ cup chopped almonds

PREHEAT THE OVEN TO 350°F. Position two oven racks in the top and bottom third of the oven. Line two baking sheets with parchment paper and set aside.

In the bowl of a stand mixer fitted with the paddle attachment, beat the sugar and butter on high speed until light and fluffy, about 5 minutes. Add the egg and beat until fully incorporated. Beat in the lemon zest, vanilla extract, and almond extract.

In a medium bowl, whisk together the flour, cornmeal, baking soda, and salt. With the mixer running on low speed, slowly add the flour mixture to the butter mixture. Remove the bowl from the mixer stand and fold in the cherries and almonds.

Put a few tablespoons of sugar in a shallow bowl.

Form tablespoon-sized balls of dough, roll in the sugar to coat, and place on the prepared baking sheets, spacing them about 1½ inches apart. Bake until the cookies are golden, 8 to 10 minutes. Remove from the oven.

These are best served warm, but the cooled cookies will keep in an airtight container for 3 to 5 days.

COOK'S NOTE: Stone-ground cornmeal is important for this recipe. Because it's a bit more granular than regular cornmeal, it adds a bit of texture and chew to the cookie.

A SWEET ENDING

ONE OF THE TRICKS I HAVE UP MY SLEEVE IS TO SERVE AN UNEXPECTED after-dessert treat. It's a works-every-time crowd-pleaser (and that's an understatement) just when everyone thinks it's time to head home. Without fail, this slightly over-the-top (in all the right ways) gesture elicits the kind of joy that comes with memories of getting to lick the batter bowl or of mugs of hot cocoa waiting for when you came in from playing in the snow. Plus you get the satisfaction of seeing guests' eyes go wide, not only because it's a complete surprise when they thought the meal was over, but also because who wouldn't want a second dessert? These recipes are all easy to make ahead and put the finishing touches on just before serving, even if you're a few glasses of wine in. Pop the cookies into the oven while your guests sip their espresso and finish off their wineglasses and then serve them hot 'n' fresh (as cookies are meant to be enjoyed). Or pass around a dish of chocolate coins. You could also tuck baked cookies or coins into pretty bags for your guests to take home, serve them alongside tea when someone stops by for a chat, or set them on a vintage plate on the bedside table for an overnight guest.

And while we're talking about bringing a lovely evening to a close, take a page from my mother-in-law's hostessing playbook. In addition to understanding the magic of the surprise after-dessert dessert and offering a round of Magnum Bars at the end of the night, she would say in her proper English accent, while motioning to a table covered with half-full glasses and a sink full of dirty dishes, "Just leave it, darling." She taught me to do as the French do—soak up the afterglow of the night and leave the cleanup effort for the morning. I've carried that laid-back attitude with me ever since, and my dinner parties are all the more pleasurable for it.

SUNDAYS

TO SLEEP IN, TO SLOW DOWN, TO SAY THANKS

Learning how to balance the constant going, going, going of work with much-needed rest is something that takes practice and lots of reminders. Sometimes you need to make an effort to steal the time for yourself if it doesn't find you naturally. Sundays offer us the perfect excuse to slow down, and I strongly suggest taking the weekly cue. To me, a balanced day well spent is one where the rhythm slows way down: sleeping in a little later, maybe eating breakfast in bed, enjoying a midday meal that lasts for hours, and catching up with one another after a busy week. What better way to spend that time than making things from scratch, like scones (page 211) or a batch of granola (page 217), or enjoying a stack of delicious pancakes (page 222) with a pitcher of warm maple syrup, baked French toast (page 229) that you can prepare almost entirely the night before, or the perfect plate of eggs (see page 232). Be gentle, be slow, be indulgent; these recipes do the work for you.

FIG & GINGER SCONES
with Salted Honey Butter

My goal for this morning treat was to create a flavor combination so tasty and unique that friends would say, "I *need* this recipe," and, well, per the numerous requests so far, I think I might have nailed it. To me, the perfect scone should be like the best part of a muffin, but with the added bonus of some sugary texture in the crust—a welcome departure from the usual dry, crumbly scone situation. From there, you can add just about anything to dot its fluffy interior; I used candied ginger and figs for this version, but see Make It Your Own for other suggestions. The best part, though, is that you can make the dough a day or two in advance, and then all you need to do is slice, bake, and serve the fresh hot scones for breakfast, with plenty of Salted Honey Butter.

FOR THE SCONES

2¼ cups all-purpose flour, plus more for dusting

⅔ cup granulated sugar

Grated zest of 1 lemon

1 tablespoon baking powder

12 tablespoons (1½ sticks) cold unsalted butter, cut into tablespoon-sized pieces

¾ cup plus 2 tablespoons heavy cream

⅓ cup candied ginger chopped into raisin-sized bits

⅓ cup dried figs chopped into raisin-sized bits

FOR THE HONEY BUTTER

8 tablespoons (1 stick) high-quality unsalted butter, at room temperature

2 tablespoons honey

¼ teaspoon Maldon salt

MAKE THE SCONES: Line a baking sheet with parchment paper and set aside.

In the bowl of a food processor, combine the flour, ⅓ cup of the sugar, lemon zest, and baking powder and pulse to combine. Add the butter and pulse until it is uniformly distributed.

Transfer the mixture to a large bowl and add ¾ cup of the cream, the candied ginger, and figs, stirring to combine. Using your hands, work the mixture into a shaggy

-recipe continues-

MAKE IT YOUR OWN: In place of the figs, you can swap in other dried fruits. These would be particularly nice with cherries, golden raisins, or currants.

dough. Turn it out onto a lightly floured surface and shape it into a log about 12 inches long and 2 inches thick.

Slice the dough into 8 rounds, each about 1½ inches thick. Place the scones on the prepared baking sheet, cover with plastic wrap, and refrigerate for at least 20 minutes, or up to 3 days.

MAKE THE BUTTER: In the bowl of a stand mixer fitted with the paddle attachment, beat the butter on high speed until light and fluffy, 3 to 5 minutes. Drizzle in half of the honey and beat to combine. Transfer the whipped butter to a decorative bowl, drizzle the remaining honey over the top, and sprinkle with the flaky salt. Set aside to serve with the warm scones.

When ready to bake the scones, preheat the oven to 375°F.

Add the remaining 2 tablespoons cream to a small bowl, and the remaining ⅓ cup sugar to another small bowl. Dunk the top of each scone in the cream, followed by the sugar, and return to the baking sheet, leaving a few inches between the scones.

Bake the scones until golden and cooked through, 15 to 18 minutes. Remove from the oven and let cool until just warm to the touch, then serve with the honey butter.

MORNING BUNS
with Pistachio & Apricot

When the occasion calls for a special-feeling breakfast, these buns should be on the menu. It's a decidedly unfussy recipe in that the deeply flavored yeasted dough can be made ahead, meaning you don't need to wake up at 4:30 a.m. to whip up an impressive fresh-out-of-the-oven spread. Your guests will assume that you were up at the crack of dawn as a proper baker would be . . . so I'll keep our secret that you really slept in.

FOR THE DOUGH

¾ cup whole milk

¼ cup granulated sugar

1 packet (2¼ teaspoons) active dry yeast

1 large egg plus 1 large egg yolk

4 tablespoons unsalted butter, melted

3 cups all-purpose flour, plus more for dusting

2 teaspoons kosher salt

Neutral oil, for the bowl

FOR THE FILLING

1½ cups toasted pistachios

¾ cup granulated sugar

1 teaspoon ground cardamom

½ teaspoon almond extract

4 tablespoons unsalted butter, at room temperature

¼ cup apricot jam

FOR THE GLAZE

½ cup granulated sugar

¼ cup honey

FOR FINISHING

2 tablespoons granulated sugar

2 tablespoons toasted pistachios, roughly chopped

MAKE THE DOUGH: In a small saucepan, heat the milk gently over medium heat, being careful not to let it come to a boil. It should be just warm to the touch, about 95°F. Transfer the milk to a small bowl, add 2 tablespoons of the sugar and the yeast, and stir to combine. Place the bowl in a warm spot and let the yeast proof for about 15 minutes; it should bubble and froth.

Whisk in the remaining 2 tablespoons sugar, the egg, and yolk until incorporated. Whisk in the melted butter and mix until fully incorporated. Switch to a wooden spoon or silicone spatula and, stirring, slowly add the flour and salt. Continue to stir until the dough comes together into a smooth ball.

Turn the dough out onto a floured surface and knead until it is soft and some-what elastic, 5 to 8 minutes. This is a nice

-recipe continues-

workout; you can use a stand mixer with the dough hook attachment, but I prefer the workout! If the dough feels too sticky, add a little flour to your work surface and knead to incorporate.

Transfer the dough to a well-oiled bowl, cover it with a cloth, and set it in a warm place to rise and double in size, 1 to 1½ hours, depending on the environment of your kitchen that day.

MAKE THE FILLING: In the bowl of a food processor, combine the pistachios, sugar, and cardamom and pulse until the mixture resembles rough sand. Add the almond extract and pulse a few times to incorporate.

Turn the dough out onto a floured surface and roll it into a 16 x 10-inch rectangle. Use your fingers to pull out each of the four corners to get a good rectangular shape. With a large spoon, spread the softened butter evenly over the dough, leaving a 1-inch border all around, followed by the apricot jam. Sprinkle the pistachio mixture evenly over the butter and jam and press it lightly into the butter and jam. Starting at a short end, tightly roll up the dough, evening out the log as you go. Trim the ends of the roll to even them.

Line a baking sheet with parchment paper. Cut the roll into 8 slices and space the buns evenly on the prepared baking sheet.

At this point, you can refrigerate the buns overnight or let them rise to bake off today. For buns today: Cover the buns with a kitchen towel and let rise for an hour or so in a warm spot. For buns tomorrow morning: Cover the buns with plastic wrap and refrigerate overnight. Let the buns come to room temperature for 30 minutes before baking.

Preheat the oven to 350°F.

Bake the buns until golden but still very moist in the middle, 10 to 12 minutes, rotating the pan halfway through to help with even baking.

MAKE THE GLAZE: In a small saucepan, combine the sugar, honey, and ½ cup water and bring to a slow simmer over medium heat, whisking until the sugar and honey have dissolved, 3 to 4 minutes. Remove from the heat and set aside in a warm spot so the glaze will still be warm when it's time to finish the buns.

FINISH THE BUNS: Brush the hot buns with the glaze, sprinkle with the sugar, and scatter the chopped pistachios on top.

BREAKFAST PANNA COTTA

Panna cotta may not be something you'd normally think of for breakfast, but this one has a twist: It's made with yogurt. The tanginess keeps it from getting too sweet while creating the ideal canvas for classic breakfast toppings like maple syrup or honey, fresh or stewed fruit, jam, or granola (especially the Rose, Cherry, and Almond Granola on page 217). It's just the dish for morning company, especially because you can prep it the night before and serve it straight from the fridge.

1½ gelatin sheets

1 cup heavy cream

2 tablespoons granulated sugar

½ vanilla bean, split lengthwise, seeds scraped out (pod discarded or saved for another use)

1½ cups plain whole-milk Greek yogurt

PUT THE GELATIN IN a shallow bowl, cover with ice water, and set aside to soak for 5 minutes to soften.

In a small saucepan, combine the cream, sugar, and vanilla and bring to a slow simmer over medium heat. Remove the pan from the heat and let the mixture cool slightly.

Remove the bloomed gelatin from the water, squeeze out the excess water, and gently stir into the cream mixture until dissolved and well combined. Fold in the yogurt, then pour the mixture into individual serving bowls and refrigerate for at least 4 hours, or overnight.

To serve, bring the panna cotta to room temperature and serve with your desired toppings.

ROSE, CHERRY & ALMOND GRANOLA

MAKES ABOUT 5 CUPS

As you probably know, homemade granola is superior to anything you can buy—toasty, complex, and sweet, but not too much so. Plus, there's a unique satisfaction that comes with reaching for the canister that you keep on the counter for easy breakfasts and snacks, or for sending some granola home with dinner guests for their own breakfasts the next day. While there is no shortage of combinations of ingredients you can dress up the recipe with, I'm especially fond of this one. The tart cherries punctuate the deeply caramelized oats and almonds, while the rose petals transform the milk or yogurt at the bottom of your bowl into the sweetest hue of soft pink.

3 cups rolled oats

¼ cup canola oil

1 large egg white

⅓ cup packed brown sugar

⅓ cup honey

½ teaspoon almond extract

¼ teaspoon ground cinnamon

¼ teaspoon kosher salt

1 cup toasted slivered almonds

1 cup dried cherries

1 cup toasted coconut

2 tablespoons dried rose petals

PREHEAT THE OVEN TO 300°F.

In a medium bowl, combine the oats, oil, egg white, brown sugar, honey, almond extract, cinnamon, and salt and stir until the oats are evenly coated. Spread the mixture out in an even layer on a baking sheet. Bake for 45 to 50 minutes, stirring every 15 minutes, until golden and toasty. Let cool completely.

Transfer the granola to a large bowl and add the almonds, cherries, coconut, and rose petals. Toss to combine. Store the granola in an airtight jar for up to 1 month.

LITTLE NUTMEG DINER DOUGHNUTS

I will never forget the day my dad bought the Ridgetop Diner. My mom drove my sister and me out to see him, and our grandparents welcomed us into the kitchen with fresh-from-the-fryer doughnuts. They were cakey in the center and fragrant with just a hint of nutmeg, and I can still taste them if I close my eyes and think back to that moment. It's a recipe that I love re-creating, and I'm still sure to serve it with a cold glass of Jersey milk.

1½ cups granulated sugar

1½ teaspoons kosher salt

1½ teaspoons baking powder

1 teaspoon freshly grated nutmeg

½ cup whole milk

1 large egg

2 tablespoons unsalted butter, melted

1 vanilla bean, split lengthwise, seeds scraped out (pod discarded or saved for another use)

2 cups all-purpose flour, plus more for dusting

Neutral oil, such as canola or vegetable, for deep-frying

IN A LARGE BOWL, whisk together ½ cup of the sugar with the salt, baking powder, and nutmeg. Add the milk, egg, melted butter, and vanilla seeds and use a wooden spoon to mix until incorporated. Add the flour and mix well until the dough is uniform and smooth.

Cover the dough with plastic wrap and refrigerate for 1 hour. In a deep fryer or large deep skillet, bring a few inches of oil to 375°F.

Dust a baking sheet generously with flour and set aside. Add the remaining 1 cup of sugar to a medium bowl and set aside.

Turn out the dough onto a well-floured surface and use a rolling pin to roll it out to about a ½-inch thickness. Use a 2½-inch doughnut cutter to cut out doughnuts, dipping the cutter(s) in flour as needed to prevent sticking. Place the doughnuts on the floured baking sheet 2 inches apart. Re-roll the scraps, cut them out, and repeat to make more doughnuts; you should have a total of 10 doughnuts.

Working in batches to avoid crowding, gently drop the doughnuts into the hot oil (the oil temperature will drop too much if you overcrowd the fryer, and you'll end up with soggy, greasy doughnuts). Fry on the first side for about 1 minute, until golden brown, then flip and cook for another minute or so, until golden brown on the second side. Transfer the fried doughnuts to the bowl of sugar and toss to coat, then arrange on a serving platter.

Serve the doughnuts fresh and hot, with tall glasses of cold milk, if you like.

SUNDAY SKILLET CAKES
{aka the Perfect Pancakes}

Being a mom, and a single mom at that, has made for a challenging and unpredictable road. But one solace that I have always held onto is that Sunday marks the beginning of a new week, a fresh start, and a chance to try again. Whenever there's been a week when I'm feeling particularly short of hitting the Mom of the Year mark, I make a batch of these fluffy pancakes with crisp buttery edges for Jaim. Watching his delight as he devours them makes the world in that moment feel entirely perfect. And we are OK.

1½ cups all-purpose flour

2 tablespoons powdered sugar

1 tablespoon baking powder

1 teaspoon kosher salt

1¼ cups buttermilk (well shaken before measuring, see Cook's Note)

1 large egg

3 tablespoons unsalted butter, melted and slightly cooled, plus more for cooking

1 teaspoon vanilla extract

Softened salted butter, for serving

Maple syrup, warmed, for serving

IN A MEDIUM BOWL, whisk together the flour, powdered sugar, baking powder, and salt. Set aside.

In another medium bowl, whisk together the buttermilk, egg, melted butter, and vanilla. Slowly whisk in the flour mixture, mixing until smooth.

Heat a large cast-iron skillet or griddle over low heat for about 5 minutes. Add a tablespoon of butter to the pan and swirl it around to coat. (The butter should sizzle slightly when it hits the pan.) Using a measuring cup, drop ¼-cup scoops of batter into the pan, leaving an inch or two between the cakes. Let cook undisturbed until the edges start to bubble, about 2 minutes. Flip each cake and cook for another 2 minutes, until golden brown around the edges and cooked through the center. Continue cooking the remaining batter in batches.

Serve immediately, with softened butter and maple syrup.

COOK'S NOTE: The trick with pancakes is finding the sweet spot on your stove—not too hot, not too cool. And don't worry, the first round is almost always a throw-away—its job is to season the pan!

If you don't happen to have buttermilk hanging around your refrigerator on a Sunday morning, whole milk will do just fine and life will go on. For a polished presentation, serve the maple syrup in a vintage creamer or pretty teapot.

MAKE IT YOUR OWN: Pancake batter is made for riffing—add an ever-so-small pinch of grated nutmeg or ground cinnamon to the batter. Or sprinkle a few blueberries or raspberries onto the uncooked side of each pancake before you flip them.

POPOVERS
with Roasted Rhubarb Jam Butter

This is the handy popover recipe that you need for your Sundays, your holidays, your life. These are not-too-sweet baked eggy puffs, and they don't need anything else except maybe a knob of butter and a smear of jam—or a combination of the two.

FOR THE ROASTED RHUBARB JAM BUTTER

½ cup rhubarb chopped into ¼-inch pieces

½ tablespoon granulated sugar

8 tablespoons (1 stick) unsalted butter, at room temperature

½ teaspoon Maldon salt

FOR THE POPOVERS

1½ cups whole milk

4 large eggs, at room temperature

2 teaspoons powdered sugar

1 teaspoon kosher salt

3 tablespoons unsalted butter, melted

1½ cups all-purpose flour

Vegetable oil, for the pan

MAKE THE JAM BUTTER: In a small bowl, combine the rhubarb and sugar. Let the mixture sit for 30 minutes to macerate.

Preheat the oven to 425°F.

Transfer the rhubarb mixture, including all the juices, to a rimmed baking sheet and spread in an even layer. Roast until the rhubarb is just tender, about 8 minutes. Set aside to cool completely.

In the bowl of a stand mixer fitted with the paddle attachment, beat the butter on high speed, scraping down the sides of the bowl now and again, until light and fluffy, 4 to 5 minutes. Reduce the mixer speed to low, add the rhubarb, along with any roasting juices, and the salt and mix until just incorporated. Set aside (or store in an airtight container in the refrigerator for up to 1 week; bring to room temperature before serving).

MAKE THE POPOVERS: In a small saucepan, gently warm the milk over low heat until just lukewarm to the touch. Remove the pan from the heat.

COOK'S NOTE: I like using a 12-mold pan for these, but you can opt for a 6-mold pan to make 6 extra-large popovers.

In a blender, combine the warm milk, eggs, powdered sugar, and salt and blend until smooth. Add the melted butter and blend until incorporated, then add the flour and blend until the batter is smooth and frothy. Let the batter rest for 15 minutes.

Preheat the oven to 450°F. Place an empty popover pan in the oven to heat for at least 5 minutes.

Remove the hot pan from the oven and carefully brush or spray each cup with vegetable oil. Divide the rested batter evenly among the popover cups, filling them about three-quarters full.

Bake the popovers for 20 minutes, without opening the oven door. Reduce the heat to 350°F and bake for an additional 10 minutes, or until the popovers have "popped" over the tops of the pan and are a deep golden brown. Remove from the oven.

If you like a drier popover, pierce the top of each one with the tip of a paring knife to release steam and return the popovers to the oven for another minute. If you like your popover more custardy (like Yorkshire pudding), do not pierce them. Serve immediately, with the roasted rhubarb butter.

FRESH SQUEEZED IS BEST

THERE IS NOTHING BETTER THAN SWIGS
of fresh citrus juice in the morning.
Go with traditional navel oranges, or
try clementines or Cara Cara oranges.
The color will be bold and the flavor
a delicious surprise.

CHERRY & ALMOND BAKED FRENCH TOAST

My mom would occasionally make what felt like fancy French toast, soaking it overnight in the fridge so it would get rich and custardy as it baked the next morning. It was like starting the day off with dessert, which made an unremarkable Sunday feel like a holiday. This recipe continues to be in my rotation—with the slight update of cherries and almonds—because I only need to throw it into the oven in the morning, and there's nothing more luxurious on the weekend than time.

⅔ cup granulated sugar

½ cup dried cherries

8 (1-inch-thick) slices good bread, such as challah, brioche, or crusty sourdough

1 cup apricot jam

Softened unsalted butter, for the pan

¾ cup heavy cream

2 large eggs

2 large egg yolks

2 teaspoons almond extract

2 teaspoons vanilla extract

2 teaspoons grated orange zest

¾ teaspoon kosher salt

¼ cup slivered almonds

Warm maple syrup, for serving

IN A SMALL SAUCEPAN, combine ⅓ cup of the sugar and ⅓ cup water and bring to a boil over medium heat. Remove the pan from the heat and add the cherries. Let sit for 10 minutes to allow the cherries to plump and infuse with flavor. Drain the cherries, discarding the liquid, and set aside.

Cut the slices of bread in half diagonally to create triangular pieces. Slather one side of each piece with the apricot jam and set aside on a platter or tray.

Butter a baking dish large enough to hold the bread in one or two layers (I like using something pretty that can go from oven to table). Set aside.

In a medium bowl, whisk together the cream, the remaining ⅓ cup sugar, the eggs and yolks, almond extract, vanilla extract, orange zest, and salt. Place each piece of bread in the custard mixture, jam side facing up, giving it a moment to soak up some of the custard before transferring it to the baking dish (jam side up), slightly overlapping the slices in the baking dish. Scatter the cherries around and over the bread. Cover the dish with plastic wrap and refrigerate for at least 6 hours, or up to overnight.

Preheat the oven to 375°F.

Sprinkle the slices of bread with the slivered almonds and bake, uncovered, until puffy and golden, 15 to 18 minutes. Serve immediately, with warm maple syrup.

A GOOD EGG

WHEN YOUR INGREDIENTS SHINE, YOUR COOKING WILL SHINE, AND IT DOESN'T get more foundational than a good egg. When I first met my now-husband Michael, he was living on the Upper West Side of New York City in an apartment above a major chain grocery store. Whenever I visited him there, I would marvel at the ease and convenience of having a supermarket *in the same building*. The luxury! For me, the closest market was an hour-drive round-trip, and shopping often took up the better half of a day. So, out of necessity, many of us rural Mainers grow and raise a lot of our own food—including our eggs.

One morning, while making breakfast in Michael's kitchen, I cracked one of his supermarket eggs into a bowl. Seeing the pale, watery yolk I gained a much bigger appreciation for a lifetime of tending to chicken coops and for eggs I knew had been laid that morning, with big, brilliantly orange yolks the color of persimmons that stood up proud and tall on top of the whites. *I* was the one with the luxury. I'll never forget the morning I pulled a just-laid egg from our coop here in Maine and placed it in Michael's hand. His eyes went wide with amazement—"Hot from the hen!" And when he saw that vibrant goldenrod yolk get whisked into a simple scramble and tasted how rich it was without any cheese or cream added, he too wanted to be spoiled with good eggs for life. We've been raising a flock of egg hens together ever since.

It brings us both a lot of satisfaction, watching them peacefully peck about our little plot of land each morning, searching for grubs and sweet grass to nibble on—the secret ingredients for a healthy yolk. Watching them flit about the yard, I can almost feel my blood pressure drop; it's like gazing at fish swimming lazily about in an aquarium. And the eggs they produce—what joy! Their shells can be anywhere from rich chocolate brown to robin's-egg blue to an olive green that doesn't look possible to have come from nature. And, of course, there are the eggs, begging to be served as unadorned as possible, needing nothing but a sprinkle of salt.

You don't need to raise your own chickens to get high-quality eggs—although, if you have a little patch of grass and you're inclined, I strongly recommend it!—but it is worth your while to investigate how to get the freshest eggs possible. A local farmers' market will most likely have what you're looking for. I promise, once you crack one of those delicious eggs into your bowl, you'll never look back.

How to Tell the Freshness of an Egg

Submerge your eggs in a large bowl of water. Fresh eggs will lie on their sides on the bottom of the bowl, completely submerged. Slightly older but still perfectly good eggs will stand on end on the bottom of the bowl but will stay submerged. Old eggs will float. Discard them.

Cooking the Perfect Egg

Once you've found your good eggs, you've got a duty to cook them well. Here are a few tips and rules of thumb for perfectly cooked eggs, any way you like 'em.

BOILED EGGS

First of all, an egg myth: Old eggs peel better. I've disproven this by cooking an egg that was laid within the hour and had a perfectly peelable egg. It's all in the cooking technique.

Don't start the eggs by submerging them in a pot of cold water and bringing it to a boil on the stove. This is where you've been going wrong. First, let your eggs come to room temperature, which will keep them from cracking when they hit the hot water. Next, bring a pot of water to a rolling boil, then gently add the eggs to the boiling water. Set a timer for the desired doneness and let them cook at a boil. Drain and peel. Cooked this way, the eggs will behave perfectly for you.

Soft-boiled (runny yolk): 6 minutes	Medium-boiled (just-set yolk): 7 minutes	Hard-boiled (firmly set yolk): 8 minutes

The timing can, of course, depend on the size of your eggs and how many you've added to the pot at one time. If you have nest-run eggs fresh from a farm, meaning they haven't been sorted and sized, they are sure to vary, so take that into account and adjust accordingly.

FRIED EGGS

Cast iron is your best friend here. A properly seasoned cast-iron pan will make all of the difference between a fried egg that sticks and one that gets perfectly golden around the edges of the whites and does not stick. Start with a very

low flame. Add a knob of butter; the butter will start to bubble. As the bubbles grow larger and start to slow, the foam will start to subside. Don't let the butter brown. Crack your egg into a shallow bowl (to ensure that no shells get into the pan), then gently drop the egg into the pan. Let it do its thing. To make a perfect sunny-side-up egg, just let it be for about 2 minutes, until the white has turned opaque and the yolk has set just slightly. Or, if you prefer an over-easy egg, flip it with confidence after 2 minutes and cook for another minute. I weirdly love to use a fish spatula for this task. It works very well.

POACHED EGGS

Fill a large skillet three-quarters full with water and bring it to a rolling boil. Use a large spoon to quickly stir the water to create a whirlpool and gently crack the eggs (I like to do 3 at a time) into the middle of the whirlpool. Be prepared—one egg almost always goes rogue. After 3 minutes, use a slotted spoon to remove the cooked eggs, pausing briefly to let any excess water drain back into the skillet, and transfer to a plate or kitchen towel to drain briefly.

SCRAMBLED EGGS

Once again, the key is a well-seasoned cast-iron pan. Set your flame on low and let the skillet hang out on the flame for a few minutes. Meanwhile, crack the eggs into a shallow bowl. Season with a pinch of salt, which helps break down the proteins in the eggs and will make the eggs fluffier. Whisk the eggs vigorously until they turn a bit paler and bubbles start to form. Add a knob of butter to the warm pan and swirl it around. Just as the bubbles start to subside, add the eggs and let them sit for a second. When you see the edges start to set, use a silicone spatula to move the eggs around in the pan. Let them sit again briefly, then turn them once again with the spatula. Turn the heat off and turn the eggs once more. Keep in mind that scrambled eggs should still be slightly wet in the middle, because they will continue to cook as they sit. My favorite way to serve these? With a sprinkle of chopped fresh chives.

SUNDAY SUPPERS

BREAKFAST ISN'T THE ONLY MEAL THAT GETS A LITTLE MORE SPECIAL WHEN we slow way down on the weekend. Growing up, I always looked forward to the Sunday suppers my grandparents or my mom would make for us. They'd start cooking in the morning, maybe getting a pork roast into the oven or boiling a corned beef, taking a little bit longer to prepare a meal that wouldn't be practical on a weeknight, when my mom was rushing in from work or my dad was coming home after spending a zillion hours at the diner. There was a subtle but distinct shift in the air, as there was nowhere to be but exactly where we were. We weren't cooking because of mouths to feed and bedtimes to hit, but because of the pure pleasure of it. And then, when the meal was ready midday, that's when we'd eat—because why wait? We'd sit and eat and drink and visit and just *breathe*. It was the most relaxed I remember being as a kid (which is saying a lot; our house wasn't exactly relaxing), and it's something I want everyone to be able to experience. The sheer indulgence of *"My one job today is to eat at 1 p.m."*

So this is your reminder to embrace the break from routine, the time you have with your family and the people you care about the most, and the slowing down of time that we don't often get. The easiest and most enjoyable way to do that is to cook something delicious, and to do it with intention and presence of mind. Any of the recipes in this book will do right by you.

SIGNATURES

All my life I've been figuring out how to do a lot with a little. From the time I was very young, the fields and forests and streams were my playground, and my whole world was finding treasures in the details. I used that resourcefulness when I opened the doors to my supper club, taking advantage of the bounty that surrounded me to fill in the gaps of what I couldn't buy with money (which was most things). I foraged (both outdoors and in antique shops and secondhand stores); I got creative with humble materials, elevating them with my finds; and I made what I could with my own two hands. I clipped forsythia and pear tree branches and forced the blossoms for impressively dramatic arrangements; I used balsam, spruce, elderflowers, and lilacs to infuse simple syrups and teas; and I gathered flowers such as bachelor's buttons, cosmos, phlox, and bolted herb blossoms to sprinkle over dishes. I filled empty wine bottles with ferns and turned them into candle holders, draped painters' drop cloths from the hardware store over rickety tables, nestled oysters into beds of chilled rocks and moss, and made place settings with platters, plates, glasses, and silverware imbued with the memories of everyone who'd used them before me. None of this changed when I opened The Lost Kitchen or could finally afford new plates; in fact, I leaned even further into it. Because what I learned over the years is that those details—while born out of necessity—are what made the evenings in my home, and now make my restaurant, so special. Yes, people remember the food. But it's the small moments and touches that make them feel like they are experiencing something extraordinary.

This chapter is devoted to the unique signatures that can set you and your meals apart. None of these take much time, and certainly not much money. But they do take thoughtfulness—and that's the point. With a little advance planning (and maybe a pair of pruning shears), you'll have everything you need to treat your guests, and yourself, to a little something special.

BRING THE OUTSIDE IN

AT THE CENTER of The Lost Kitchen are flowers and other botanicals, like branches and moss—seeing them, smelling them, feeling them, and eating or drinking them. That's because I am always looking to bring more of the outside in. It roots my food in a sense of place, brings the seasons directly to the table, stirs the senses, and connects with memory in the powerful way that nature does so well. Not to mention the fact that the results are beautiful. And they come from right outside my front door. So it should be no surprise that many of these signatures fall into two categories devoted entirely to doing just that: Eat More Flowers and Live with Flowers.

Eat More Flowers

When I was cooking at my dad's diner, there were years that would go by without the menu changing one bit. That was part of the beauty of the place, knowing that it was a reliable standby where you could always get a cup of chowder, a juicy burger, or a hot chicken sandwich slathered in gravy on pillow-soft white bread. But eventually I started yearning for a change; I wanted to put my stamp on some of our staple dishes. I knew my dad would never go for it, so I started small, sneaking some nasturtiums I'd gathered from my mother's garden onto our signature lobster roll. I peeked through the pickup window as the waitresses grabbed the plates to go out to the diners, then watched as our regulars took in this new floral addition to their lunches. I saw that moment of delight, occasionally mixed with a little confusion, pass over their faces before they tucked in. Without saying a word, I had communicated something deep and personal to them. And so my obsession with edible blossoms was born.

Edible flowers can come from a variety of places, whether you grow them in a garden, find them flourishing on their own in the wild, or wait for your herbs to bolt and go to flower. No matter where you forage them from, sprinkle these blossoms deliberately, liberally, and with love.

FROM THE GARDEN

These are some of my favorite varieties that are easy to grow on your own or seek out from your favorite farmer:

NASTURTIUMS: sweet, peppery, zesty

PANSIES AND VIOLETS: delicate, sweet, lettuce-y

MARIGOLDS: bitter with notes of citrus and tarragon

BORAGE: tastes like cucumber, salt, and honey

ROSES: floral with hints of strawberry and apples

FORGET-ME-NOTS: mild and grassy

BACHELOR'S BUTTONS: sweet and peppery with a hint of cucumber

PHLOX: mild, bitter, fragrant

DIANTHUS: floral with notes of celery and clove

COSMOS: nectar-like sweetness with notes of mango and a zesty finish

CALENDULA: sweet, floral, bitter

GARLIC CHIVES: pungent; like a blend of garlic and onion

CALIFORNIA POPPIES: bitter, warm, aromatic

GO WILD

Look around with fresh eyes—whether it's in your backyard or the woods, chances are you'll find at least one of these gems that would make a beautiful surprise on your table.

CEDAR, BALSAM, AND SPRUCE TIPS: In the winter, this is where I find green. Use these as a winter substitute for rosemary, make into syrups for cocktails (see page 53) or sorbets (see page 56), steep them into teas, or slip them into hot skillets filled with mussels or scallops and lots of butter.

FORSYTHIA: When these branches are in bloom in spring, their yellow flowers are like sunshine bursting into the backyard. Use them to make a syrup to glaze cakes or steep them into tea (see page 248). And when you're really in need of that sunshine, you can gather the branches and force the blooms for a gorgeous sculptural arrangement (see page 252).

ELDERFLOWERS: I have a little bush outside the restaurant that's my compass for the seasons—it's officially summer when the elderflowers pop. I scramble down the rocks by the waterfall to harvest them by the bucketful and use them to make syrups to glaze cakes or sweeten cordials (page 53), or I batter and deep-fry them for a fun twist on a state-fair treat.

LILACS: These are my dad's favorite flower. They bloom around his birthday, and I always knew that if there was nothing else that I could give him that would make him happy, there was always a bouquet of lilacs. It's that signature spring smell when you roll down the windows of the car, take a big inhale, and know the gray fog of winter has lifted. Somehow, magically, it's possible to bottle that by using the blooms to make syrups for sorbets (see page 56) and cocktails (see page 53), or infuse them into vinegar (see page 158).

WILD STRAWBERRY BLOSSOMS: Every summer I find these tiny blossoms growing right in my lawn. They rarely produce fruit (thanks to the lawnmower), but they make the sweetest garnish for desserts and cheese plates.

APPLE, CHERRY, AND PEAR BLOSSOMS: Come spring, when the first little white flowers emerge, you can spot these in your yard, your neighbor's yard, the park, or the roadside. They're so delicate that they dissolve in your mouth, and I love using them in surprising ways like sprinkling them on cheeseburgers (especially when we make the burgers with the beef we get from a farmer who finishes her cows on fermented apples).

WILD BLACKBERRY BLOSSOMS: There is nothing sweeter or more in the spirit of summer than the blossoms from a wild blackberry bush. Use them to garnish desserts or cheese plates.

BOLTED AND BEAUTIFUL

If you've ever let your garden go a little (or a lot), you know how what began as a tidy little plot or pot of herbs or vegetables can quickly become a jungle of tall, unruly plants that have bolted. In that wildness is the gift of their blossoms, which are not only beautiful but also taste faintly of the herb or vegetable itself. When dotted on top of dishes, they feel special and rare. My favorite examples of these are:

CILANTRO: tiny white flowers

RADISH: soft pink-and-white flowers

BROCCOLI AND BRASSICAS: sweet yellow flowers

ARUGULA: tiger-striped soft yellow flowers

OREGANO: purple tufts of flowers

MINT: delicate purple fluffs

DILL: soft green fireworks

FENNEL: bright yellow fireworks that look like they've been kissed with bee pollen (which is actually fennel pollen)

CHIVES: purple bursts with pure oniony flavor (I love them dipped into a light tempura batter and deep-fried; they're like the tiniest, and prettiest, "blooming onions" you've ever had)

MAKE FRESH TEA

Steeping herbs and flowers in hot water for tea is as effortless as it is gorgeous and rewarding. Serve the tea hot for a cozy mugful or iced on days when you (and your guests) need a refreshing treat. And definitely take creative freedom with blending flavors together. Here are some of my favorites:

Peony petals

Rose petals

Fresh mint

Fresh thyme

Fresh rosemary

Spruce tips

Fresh lavender

Fresh chamomile

TO MAKE THE TEA: Add the herbs or flowers to a teapot or jar and top off with hot water. (My rule of thumb is to do a heaping handful of botanicals to every cup of water.) Let steep for at least 3 to 4 minutes.

If using a jar, strain the tea and serve. Otherwise, let your guests pour as they please.

Live with Flowers

There is no easier, or less expensive, way to lift your mood, connect with joy, and surround yourself with beautiful things than to invite more flowers (or nature in general) into your home. You would be hard-pressed to find a room of mine, in my house or in the restaurant, without at least a bud vase. From the time I was a little girl, bringing home flowers was a compulsion. I'd gather blooms from the fields or my mom's garden, leaves and moss and branches from the forest, and, as I got older, whatever I could get my hands on along the roadside. I was drawn to the magic of these things—as most people are.

You could spend all the money in the world on fancy dishes and linens, but the result would still pale in comparison to the spray of hydrangea you clipped that morning or lavender you picked up at the market. Adding living things to a table or room brings warmth along with a pleasingly sensory element that you can smell and feel. They fill the room with *life*. Here you'll find some easy ways to do just that.

FORAGED FLORAL

Some of my most impressive arrangements are those that showcase flowers and other botanicals that I've found rather easily. Try these:

FORSYTHIA BRANCHES

ELDERFLOWER BRANCHES

LILAC BRANCHES

FLOWERING FRUIT TREE BRANCHES, SUCH AS APPLE, PEAR, CHERRY, QUINCE, PEACH, OR PLUM

FERNS

CEDAR BRANCHES

ROADSIDE LUPINE

QUEEN ANNE'S LACE

GOLDENROD

FORCE NATURE

In the late days of winter, it can sometimes feel like spring will never arrive. In these moments, we need to take time into our own hands. By clipping certain types of branches and placing them in warm water, you can "force" the buds to bloom. Apple, pear, peach, quince, and forsythia branches are all suitable for this neat trick, which then serves as a powerful reminder that spring is not too far away. Immerse the branches in a favorite vase filled with warm water. Within a week or two, tiny buds will begin to emerge, followed by a spray of blossoms. You can lightly pound the cut ends of the branches with a hammer before submerging them in the water, which will help them soak up even more of the warmth. Replenish the warm water daily to speed things up.

DON'T FORGET BRANCHES

When there are no flowers available anywhere, especially in the dead of winter, don't overlook the power of bare branches and twigs. A big vase full of them adds drama to a room. Or use tiny hooks in your ceiling to hang bundles for an upside-down tablescape. I particularly like elderflower branches for this because of how dramatic and sculptural they look.

COLLECTING VASES

It becomes a lot easier to create floral arrangements when you have a small trove of vases at the ready. I'm always on the hunt for different ones to add to the collection that sits next to my kitchen sink so I will have a variety of shapes, sizes, and heights to accommodate whatever I've foraged. Here are some things to keep in mind:

Tall, clear, cylindrical vases are perfect for filling with enormous branches and making a real statement. Or add a slender birch log (about 1½ inches wide, cut to length) so it will anchor the vase with weight. Maple sap buckets, large antique pitchers, and cast-iron urns work well too.

Tiny bud vases make for sweet little touches on the table or tucked into unexpected places, like next to the bathroom sink. Recycled bottles, such as those from maple syrup, clear wine bottles, or vintage Coke bottles all make for charming bud vases.

Wide-mouth vases make it easier to cluster larger blooms or branches, like hydrangeas, peonies, lilacs, and forsythia.

CRYSTAL CLEAR

When using clear glass vases, add a few drops of bleach to the flower water (or a capful for an extra-large vase). The bleach will kill any unwanted organic bacteria that could turn the water murky, yet it's diluted enough to let your flowers or branches thrive.

CHILL

Refrigerate arrangements at night before you go to bed; they like the cold and will last longer. Pull them out in the morning and enjoy them throughout your day. If your refrigerator can't afford the space, use a cool room or basement instead. On chilly autumn and spring days, I store flowers overnight in my mudroom, which will keep them happier-looking for at least a week.

THE MAGIC OF MOSS

I have a slight obsession with moss. There is something that it sparks inside me when I see it in the woods or along the road. Maybe it evokes childhood memories of playing in the backwoods of our farmland, stepping on the soft tufts next to the stream with my bare feet, pretending that the moss was a carpet and the woods were my home. Now I love finding ways to bring it to the table. Whether you have moss near where you live or find it at the local nursery, here are ways to highlight its lush, organic softness:

- Use it as a bed alongside frozen rocks when plating oysters. It makes it look as though you just happened upon those oysters, wild and free, nestled just like this.

- Arrange some down the center of your table—who needs a cloth runner when you've got moss?

- For a unique presentation, fill a bowl with moss and top it with hard-boiled eggs with a side of flaky sea salt for dipping.

- Use moss to cover the soil around potted houseplants to make them look like they've just been harvested from the forest. Mist the moss with a plant mister to keep it alive.

WHEAT BERRIES IN WINTER

Another inexpensive winter botanical standby for me are wheatberries. Although you'd normally cook and eat them as a grain, if you sprout them, you can have sweet little blades of greenery on your table—even sweeter if you get creative with your pot of choice, such as a vintage teacup.

WHAT YOU'LL NEED

A decorative pot, vase, or teacup

A bit of potting soil

A tablespoon or so of wheat berries (or farro)

Fill the pot with soil, leaving 2 inches empty at the top. Sprinkle the soil with the wheat berries (or farro), then cover with another inch of soil. Moisten the soil with water and place the pot in a warm, sunny place (the warmest and sunniest you can manage). Water as needed. You should see sprouts within 4 to 5 days.

FORAGED CANDLES

Instead of recycling your empty clear-glass wine bottles, use them as candle holders. Soak each bottle in warm, soapy water to remove the label, then slip a flower, branch, fern frond, or bundle of herbs inside it. Then add a tapered candle to the mouth of the bottle.

SETTING THE SCENE

THERE MAY BE one thing that I enjoy even more than preparing a meal, and that's setting the table. Maybe it's an appreciation for that quiet moment before the kitchen starts humming at full throttle when I can start to channel the kind of experience I want my guests to have that evening. Or maybe it's because I get to play with all of my favorite dishes, platters, tablecloths, runners, candlesticks, glasses, and silverware. In any case, I put the same love and intention into setting the table as I do into cooking the meal. The food may be the moment, but the table is what holds the spaces in between courses, where laughter and conversation and big or little thoughts intermingle to become our memories.

These are my suggestions for how to set a table with heart. Just remember that a good table is like a well-loved home—it isn't furnished overnight. It takes years of thoughtfully collecting pieces that mean something. Good things take good time.

- **FORGET THE RULES.** This isn't Emily Post. The warmest, most beautiful tables aren't those that have all the correct silverware, although you do need some silverware (at least most of the time). Maybe people judge me for it when they come to the restaurant, but what I use to guide my table-setting is what people will need to feel comfortable: somewhere to put their food, something to eat it with, napkins, a small vase of flowers, candles for soft light, small bowls for Maldon salt and freshly ground black pepper (or a small pepper grinder), and a corkscrew. OK, fine, one rule: Don't go to all the trouble of setting a nice table only to put out some cheapo corkscrew. Make it one you care about.

- **TELL A STORY WITH THE PLATES.** Vintage and antique plates wield the power of their past lives. I love thinking about where they've been and who they've fed (and what!). I often mix them in with contemporary dishes for a more personal touch. I find that a table is much more inviting when everything isn't perfectly uniform and new.

- **THERE'S BEAUTY IN PATINA.** I love collecting vintage silverware and glassware because when it's mixed and matched, the restaurant actually feels like someone's home—which it should! The warmth of worn items lets your guests know that they can relax and be themselves. Plus, beautiful old things tend to always look good together no matter which pieces you choose.

- **BUILD A COLLECTION OF CANDLE-STICKS.** There is no better mood lighting for a meal than candlelight. You'll rarely find me using anything else, other than maybe a few small lamps. I am always looking for interesting candlesticks to add into my rotation, from wrought iron to brass to ceramic. Mismatched old brass candlesticks are abundant in vintage and antique shops, and they look great in clusters. Try to find different-sized taper candles as well, to create visual interest.

- **BRING PEOPLE TOGETHER WITH PLATTERS.** I am partial to serving my dishes, especially salads and main courses, on platters because that way, people need to interact to serve themselves or one another. And the visual of a pretty platter heaped with something delicious is the fastest way to make a table look like the place you want to be. I like searching antique shops and tag sales for pieces with character. Look for patterns that call to you; you'll be surprised at how strong the tug is on your memories. And don't mind a crack or a chip; it's just a sign of a life well lived.

- **MIX MEDIUMS.** When choosing items for your table, think about blending textures and materials, such as wood, slate, porcelain, marble, brass, iron, and ceramic. Keeping everything one-note can seem cold and sterile.

- **BE A TABLECLOTH RENEGADE.** My general rule is to never use a tablecloth on an inside table and to almost always use one when eating outside. I think that a tablecloth lends too formal a feel to an inside table, but outside, the opposite is true. I love the surprise factor of using such a "fancy" touch for wildly casual occasions, like a picnic table at the lobster pound or lunch on the back of a fishing boat. The idea is almost humorous and always evokes a smile.

- **DROP EVERYTHING.** An inexpensive but durable canvas painter's drop cloth can serve a number of purposes, and it looks elegant yet rustic when dressed up with your place settings. Cut one down for a tablecloth or runner, or use it as a picnic blanket.

- **PUT YOUR ENERGIES INTO IRONED NAPKINS INSTEAD OF FORMAL TABLE LINENS.** They don't merely have to be useful; they can also add to the experience. Pour a few capfuls of rosewater into your steam iron when you press them, and they'll bring a welcome surprise whenever guests dab their faces.

FOAMING ROSE SILVER POLISH

I came up with this rose-scented soak-and-scrub recipe after looking for a slightly more special way to polish my vintage silverware finds. If yours is like mine and looks like it's seen many meals, why not spoil it? It's been through a lot.

¼ cup baking soda

¼ cup kosher salt

1 tablespoon dried rose petals

2 cups white vinegar

LINE A 9 X 13-INCH baking pan with foil and put your silver in it in a single layer.

In a medium bowl, stir together the baking soda, salt, and rose petals. Sprinkle the mixture evenly over the silverware. Slowly pour the vinegar over the top; it will react and bubble. Give the pan a shake to distribute the soak and let rest for 10 minutes.

Remove a piece of silverware from the bath and scrub it with a polishing cloth. Rinse with hot water and polish dry. Repeat with the remaining silver.

KITCHEN HAND SCRUB

A day's work in the kitchen deserves a relaxing, luxurious ending—even if that's just washing your hands. Keep a jar of this near your kitchen sink, or take one with you as a gift for the host or hostess.

¾ cup granulated sugar

1 tablespoon poppy seeds

⅓ cup vegetable oil

1 teaspoon essential oil, such as rose, geranium, rosemary, or lavender

1 teaspoon vitamin E oil

IN A SMALL BOWL, mix all of the ingredients until well combined. Transfer to a jar with a tight-fitting lid, and use a scoop of the scrub whenever you wash your hands.

TLK HACKS

I'm always thinking about ways I can send people home with a piece of The Lost Kitchen. The recipes in this book are, of course, a great start, as are any of these "hacks" that we've learned and leaned on over the years.

Chilled Mist

I like offering my guests a spritz of a refreshing floral or herbal mist on hot days. We "serve" these in plant misters and let our guests spritz to their hearts' content. Some of my go-to flowers and herbs for this are rosemary, roses, thyme, and peonies.

WHAT YOU'LL NEED

½ cup packed flowers or herbs

IN A SMALL SAUCEPAN, bring 4 cups water to a boil over medium-high heat. Remove the pan from the heat and add the flowers or herbs. Let the mixture steep for 2 hours, then strain and chill. The infusion will keep in the fridge for up to 1 week.

Homemade Picks

Serve these beautiful foraged toothpicks with nibbles and cheese plates, use as skewers for drink garnishes, or thread with chicken, shrimp, or vegetables for kebabs. I like using maple twigs for this because they're usually available in abundance (and they are not poisonous), but you could also use apple or pear.

WHAT YOU'LL NEED

Maple twigs (or other nonpoisonous twigs), about ¼ inch thick

USE PRUNING SHEARS TO trim the twigs into just the right size for your use: about 4 inches for appetizer or cheese picks, or 6 inches for kebabs or grilling skewers. Use a pencil sharpener to whittle one end of each twig to a point.

Cold Cloths for a Hot Day

MAKES 12 CLOTHS

When I first opened the restaurant, it didn't have air-conditioning. And our Maine summers aren't exactly forgiving. As a particularly hot July Saturday approached, I knew there would be no avoiding the heat once the dining room was filled with forty guests and four burners were blasting on the stovetop. I had to give some thought to how to keep my guests comfortable, even if Mother Nature was putting up a good fight. That was when the "cold cloth course" was born. Because not all treats from the kitchen have to be edible, this one comes in the form of small flour or cotton sack cloths that are dampened with lavender linen water, chilled, and bundled with sprigs of fresh lavender.

1 (10-ounce) bottle lavender linen water or spray

Twelve 12-inch-square cloths— heavy flour sack cotton works well here

Twelve 4- to 5-inch lengths twine

Fresh lavender sprigs, about 3 inches long

POUR THE LINEN WATER into a medium bowl and set aside.

Dampen the cloths with tap water. Lay out one cloth, wrong side up, on a clean work surface. Fold the right side over toward the center of the cloth, then repeat with the left side so the two edges meet in the center. The result should mimic a set of doors, hinged left and right and closing in the middle. Fold the right vertical "hinge" over to meet the left vertical hinge, like closing a book. Then roll up the cloth tightly and evenly from the bottom to the top.

Dip the cloth roll in the linen water and then gently squeeze out the excess moisture. Repeat with the remaining cloths.

Store the cloths in an airtight container in the refrigerator until ready to use, up to 2 days. Just before using them, loosely tie up each roll with twine, using a single knot. Gently slip a sprig of lavender beneath each knot and tighten gently to secure the sprig in place. Snip the ends of the twine to the desired length.

HOST'S NOTE: Wait to tie up the cloths with the twine until the day you plan to use them, as certain types of twine can discolor the cloth.

MAKE IT YOUR OWN: The lavender linen water can be replaced with any other scent you love, and the fresh lavender can be swapped with any other fresh, fragrant sprigs or buds you can find in your garden or the woods.

Newspaper Cones

I think the best way to serve fried fish (especially my Wednesday Night Fish Fry, page 138) or any other fried bits is wrapped in a newspaper cone, just like at a proper British chippy. It's fun and lends a sense of humor to whatever it is you're serving. I like to line mine with parchment paper so they hold up well with even the greasiest contents.

WHAT YOU'LL NEED

11-inch squares of newspaper

12-inch squares of parchment paper

FOR EACH CONE, FOLD a newspaper square in half to create a triangle. Cut along the fold to make two triangular pieces of paper. Do the same with the parchment paper squares.

Holding a newspaper triangle with the long edge of the triangle toward you and the point facing away, fold the right-hand corner toward the top point. Pull the left-hand corner up to meet the other two points so all three tips meet, then fold them down into the center of the cone to secure them. Repeat with the remaining pieces of newspaper and then the parchment.

Insert a parchment cone inside each newspaper cone, fill with something tasty, and serve.

Herb Mops

A regular ol' pastry brush will always do, but one made of bundled herbs to brush butter onto meat or fish, or syrups onto cakes, makes the preparation—and the preparer—feel a little more special. You can use any herbs you like, but these are my usual choices.

WHAT YOU'LL NEED

4 sprigs fresh rosemary

6 sprigs fresh thyme

6 sprigs fresh lavender

A bamboo skewer

A 10-inch piece of twine

ARRANGE THE HERB SPRIGS on a work surface so that the bottom ends line up. Bundle the herbs together and use kitchen shears to trim the stem end of the bundle to about 4 inches long. Starting at the bottom of the sprigs, snuggle the skewer into the center of the herbs, stopping 2 inches below the top. Wrap the twine around the base of the herbs several times, then tie off with a knot to secure and trim the ends.

Little Gadgets to Impress

I don't usually put a lot of stock into single-use gadgets, but I find myself reaching for these again and again.

MINI WAFFLE CONE MAKER: For tiny scoops of ice cream and sorbet.

LINED CANVAS PASTRY BAGS: For the Cream Puffs (page 177) and Pecorino Puffs (page 34); they're also helpful for getting yogurt neatly into small glasses for parfaits.

CRUSHED ICE MAKER: For making drinks, raw seafood, and even bowls of crudités seem more festive.

ICE CREAM/SORBET MAKER: Because nothing comes close to homemade.

KITCHEN BLOWTORCH: Yes, a blowtorch. Don't be afraid! Your crème brûlée will thank you. I use a propane torch from the hardware store.

A SHARP KNIFE: OK, it's not a gadget, but you can get where you want to go with just one good knife. I like to say a sharp knife is like a good kiss—you don't need sharp knife *skills*, just a sharp knife.

Frozen Rocks

In looking for creative new ways to bring nature into the restaurant, we discovered that not only do frozen rocks look beautiful with oysters nestled among them but also, unlike ice, they don't melt! If you don't live near a beach or terrain with suitable rocks, a gardening center will have you covered. Wash the rocks, dry them, and store in the freezer until you're ready to use them.

Plant Misters

These sweet little gardening accessories aren't just for plants! I keep a pretty metal one in my kitchen to give raw vegetables and salads that dewy fresh-from-the-garden glow as we're serving them, or for "serving" guests a chilled mist (page 266).

Vintage Silver

I've always felt that silver trays make things feel a bit royal, which is how you want people to feel when they're in your company. Using vintage silver trays to serve drinks, snacks, or even breakfast is a touch that elevates the most basic hospitality offerings.

Cheeseboard Shingles

For unconventional—and inexpensive—cheese boards, use cedar shingles from your local building supply store. I love these for casual outdoor gatherings and often plate them individually for each guest.

Maple Buckets

Galvanized maple sap buckets make wonderful beverage chillers because of their tall, narrow shape. Plus, they have a hole at the top that makes it easy to hang them on trees for outdoor gatherings.

Ice Candles

Making ice candles has become an annual tradition for me because I love how their ethereal glow lights up deepest, darkest winter.

You'll need plastic buckets, and a night that will dip below freezing. Fill the buckets about three-quarters full with water, then place them outside to freeze. Ideally, you'll end up with a solid 2 to 3 inches of ice around the edges of the buckets, with the centers not frozen solid. Bring the buckets inside to warm for about 30 minutes so the ice easily releases from the sides of the buckets. Then take the buckets back outside and use an ice pick to carefully get through any ice that's formed on the surface. Drain off any water remaining in the buckets and gently turn out the ice candle holders. Use the ice pick to make the center holes bigger, if necessary, to fit your wax candles of choice (tea lights and votives work well). Light and enjoy.

Wax Poetic

Candles and candle holders can vary in size, but you can use a vegetable peeler to trim the bottoms of candles so they better fit the holders. And if you are going to flood your dining room with candlelight, which I highly recommend, use an expired credit card or library card to scrape off any wax from your dinner table.

MOTHER KNOWS BEST

OF THE MANY LESSONS I'VE LEARNED AND GROWN FROM, IT'S THE TEACHINGS of the mothers and other maternal women in my life that have rooted themselves most deeply in my heart. These are the women who have taught me almost everything I know about what it means to love and be loved, especially when it comes to our shared language of food. I leave you here with their words of wisdom.

Make traditions. Whether it's a party you throw every season, or a special batch of cookies every Thanksgiving (like my grandmother's molasses cookies), make a standing reason to be together with ones you love, and choose a staple recipe that they will always remember as yours. It will live on for years to come and create lots of beautiful memories for all.

—MY GRANDMOTHER BARBARA

Forage for what's edible, free, and in season. Use what you've got; sometimes it's all around you. Oh... and always keep a stick of butter out on the counter.

—MY GRANDMOTHER MURIEL

If you are serving a plated meal, warm your plates in the oven on the lowest heat for 15 minutes. The extra touch of a warm plate will not only keep your food warm, but also touch your guests' hearts.

—MY MOTHER-IN-LAW JULIA

Keep a small herb garden, even if it's a container on your deck. Add some of the fresh herbs to hot melted butter and let steep for 15 to 20 minutes. The infusion of flavor will make the butter that much more delicious, perfect for folding into batters or for simply dipping steamed lobster meat.

—MY GODMOTHER, HOLLY

Always keep a small pair of pruning shears in the glove box of your car. You never know when you might see an elderflower bush, lilac tree, or spring willow tree on your drive.

—MY MOTHER, DEANNA

What matters most is not what is on the table, but who is around it and how they feel while they're there.

—ME

ACKNOWLEDGMENTS

If love is the magic ingredient that makes an experience sing, then it's no wonder why this book came out as beautifully as it did—so much heart and care was poured into every page. It took a team of unbelievably talented, creative, and dedicated people to bring it to life, and I will forever be grateful to each and every one of them.

To my amazing editor, Deb Futter, and the fabulous "Celadon-ettes," Randi Kramer, Rachel Chou, Christine Mykityshyn, Jennifer Jackson, Jaime Noven, Rebecca Ritchey, Sandra Moore, Liza Buell, and Julia Sikora, I'm beyond thankful to have such incredible publishing partners at Celadon who made the birth of this book an absolute joy.

To Anne Twomey, Erin Cahill, and Jan Derevjanik for their impeccable eye for design, and to Molly Bloom, Karen Lumley, Michelle McMillian, and Judith Sutton for keeping the production process so smooth and painless.

To my agent, Janis Donnaud, for believing in me.

To the singular photographer, Nicole Franzen, whose luscious images have infused this book with the very soul of The Lost Kitchen. And to food stylist Rebecca Jurkevich and prop stylist Suzie Myers, who turned everything they touched to gold.

To my cowriter, Rachel Holtzman, for her constant support, organization, and for just plain getting me. I feel so fortunate to have such an amazing partner and friend to put my head together with.

To Lauren Crichton, for being there every step of the way, for every moment and every detail, and for lending your expertise and grace for every fried fish taste test.

To Connor Banow, for always being one step ahead, and Carey Dube, for being my kitchen sounding board.

To Big Pete, aka "The Van Man," for moving, shaking, and never breaking a single dish.

To Sal and Steven Kydd, for sharing your home and your hearts.

To Gordon Kenyon, for lending us your peach tree grove just as it was dripping with summer fruit, and to Adrienne and Robin, for sharing your flower-filled field. Thank you for helping me share the essence of Maine with the world.

And finally, to my husband Michael, for keeping a hand on the tiller and wind in my sails. Realizing dreams with you is the greatest adventure.

INDEX

Page numbers in *italics* refer to
photographs.

Alex (Calyx Farm), 67
allium. *See also* chive(s); garlic;
    onions; shallots
    in Roasted Allium Dip, 36, *37*
almonds
    in Cherry & Almond Baked
        French Toast, 208, *228*, 229
    in Chocolate Coins with
        Candied Ginger, Almonds &
        Rose, 8, 202, *203*
    in Dried Cherry, Cornmeal &
        Almond Cookies, *172*, 204
    in Good Green Olives with
        Almonds, Honey & Rosemary,
        18, *20*, 21
    in Roasted Peach Pie with
        Almond & Fennel, *175*, 188–
        89, *190–91*
    in Rose, Cherry & Almond
        Granola, 208, 216, 217, *218–19*
apple(s)
    in Apple and Chive Mignonette,
        157
    in Apple and Thyme
        Mignonette, 25
    in Apple Cider with Ginger &
        Rosemary, 57
    blossoms, cooking with, 247
    branches, as decor, 251–52
    in Old-Fashioned Apple Walnut
        Cake, 192, *193*
apricots
    in Carrot Salad with Marinated
        Apricots & Pistachios, 88, *89*
    in Morning Buns with Pistachio
        & Apricot, 213–14, *215*
arugula, flowers of, 248
Asparagus & Tarragon Soup, *62*,
    63

bachelor's buttons, food prepared
    with, 240, 244
Backyard Biscuits, 75, 77
    with Fennel Fried Chicken &
        Strawberry-Rhubarb Sweet
        and Sour, *124*, 125–27, *128–29*
    recipe, 127
bacon. *See also* pork dishes
    in A Chowder of Mussels with
        Bacon, Leek & Lime, *74*,
        75–76
    in Napa Wedge with Bacon
        & Blue Cheese, *82*, 83
    in Potato & Lentil Soup with
        Bacon and Herbs, 72, *73*
bags, to-go, 8, 205
balsam
    Scallops with Cedar, Chorizo
        & Lime variation using, 133
    teas/simple syrups infused
        with, 240, 244
Barbara (grandmother), 277
Basic Breadcrumbs, 154
    in Green Beans with Sage,
        Garlic & Breadcrumbs, 102
    recipe, 169
basil
    Lilac Sorbet variation using, 56
    Mignonette, 157
    Sweet Cream Ice Cream
        variation using, 197
    in Thai Basil Lemonade, 18, 50,
        52, 202
    Vinaigrette, 157
Bay Leaf & Thyme Perfect Potato
    Puree, 112–13
    in Farmhouse Pie with Duck
        Confit, Roasted Grapes &
        Shallots, 146–49, *147*
beef dishes
    Garlicky Mignon Steaks with
        Caramelized Onion Butter,
        136, 137

Roasted Bone Marrow Butter
    with Chives, 8, 22, *23*, 72, 77
Beets, Honeyed, with Feta &
    Toasted Pistachios, 108, *109*
Berries, Fresh, with Cloud Whip,
    174, *182*, 183
beverages
    Apple Cider with Ginger
        & Rosemary, 57
    Fresh Fruit Shrub, *51*, 53
    juice, fresh-squeezed, 225
    maple buckets as chillers for,
        274
    silver trays for, 274
    Slush Pups, 50, *51*
    tea, 57, 179, 205, 240, 244,
        248, *249*
    Thai Basil Lemonade, 18, 50,
        52, 202
Biscuits, Backyard, 75, 77
    with Fennel Fried Chicken &
        Strawberry-Rhubarb Sweet
        and Sour, *124*, 125–27, *128–29*
    recipe, 127
blackberry(ies)
    blossoms, cooking with, 240,
        247
    in Peach & Blackberry Bread
        Salad, *90*, 91
Blueberry Mignonette, 157
Blue Cheese & Bacon with Napa
    Wedge Salad, *82*, 83
Boiled Eggs, 232
bolting of plants, 243, 248
Bone Marrow Butter, Roasted,
    with Chives, 8, 22, *23*, 72, 77
borage, food prepared with, 244
brassicas, flowers of, 248
Breadcrumbs, Basic, 154
    in Green Beans with Sage and
        Garlic, 102
    recipe, 169

ERIN FRENCH is the owner and chef of The Lost Kitchen, a forty-seat restaurant in Freedom, Maine, that was recently named one of *Time*'s World's Greatest Places and one of "12 Restaurants Worth Traveling Across the World to Experience" by *Bloomberg*. She is the author of the *New York Times* bestselling memoir *Finding Freedom* and features in Magnolia Network's *The Lost Kitchen*, which is now in its third season. A born-and-raised native of Maine, she learned early the simple pleasures of thoughtful food and the importance of gathering for a meal. Her love of sharing Maine and its delicious heritage with curious dinner guests and new friends alike has been lauded by such outlets as the *New York Times*, *Martha Stewart Living*, NPR's *All Things Considered*, *The Chew*, *CBS This Morning*, *Today*, the *Wall Street Journal*, the *Boston Globe*, and *Food & Wine*.